Communications
in Computer and Information Science   1742

More information about this series at https://link.springer.com/bookseries/7899

Rajesh Singh · Valentina Emilia Balas ·
Arpan Kumar Kar · Anita Gehlot ·
Shahab Shamshirband (Eds.)

Business Data Analytics

First International Conference, ICBDA 2022
Dehradun, India, October 7–8, 2022
Proceedings

Editors
Rajesh Singh (iD)
Uttaranchal University
Dehradun, Uttarakhand, India

Valentina Emilia Balas (iD)
Aurel Vlaicu University of Arad
Arad, Arad, Romania

Arpan Kumar Kar (iD)
Indian Institute of Technology Delhi
New Delhi, Delhi, India

Anita Gehlot (iD)
Uttaranchal University
Dehradun, Uttarakhand, India

Shahab Shamshirband (iD)
National Yunlin University of Science
and Technology
Douliu, Taiwan

ISSN 1865-0929   ISSN 1865-0937 (electronic)
Communications in Computer and Information Science
ISBN 978-3-031-23646-4   ISBN 978-3-031-23647-1 (eBook)
https://doi.org/10.1007/978-3-031-23647-1

This Springer imprint is published by the registered company Springer Nature Switzerland AG
The registered company address is: Gewerbestrasse 11, 6330 Cham, Switzerland

Preface

The Uttaranchal University, Dehradun, Uttarakhand, India organized the International Conference on Business Data Analytics (ICBDA 2022) on October 7–8, 2022. The purpose of conference was to bring the diverse community of experts in data science, machine learning, and analytics from all over the world to share their original research. The theme of the conference included three subcategories: Predictive Modelling and Data Analytics, Decision Analytics and Support Systems, and Business data Analytics.

The organizing committee is extremely grateful to the authors who showed a tremendous response to the call for papers. From the 107 papers that were submitted from researchers, academicians, and students, six papers were selected for publication in this volume in Springer's CCIS series. Each submission was reviewed by at least three members of the Technical Program Committee in a single-blind process to ensure the high quality of the conference proceedings.

We are obliged to our Honorable Chancellor Shri Jitendra Joshi, Vice Chancellor Dharam Buddhi, Vice President Satbir Sehgal, and Pro-Vice Chancellor Rajesh Bahuguna for the confidence they invested in us as we organized this international conference. We are grateful to the conveners of the conference Dean Pradeep Suri and Dean Sonal Sharma, the organizing secretary, all faculty members and staff on different committees for organizing the conference and making it a grand success. We extend our thanks to the authors of the conference papers without them it would not be possible to publish quality papers.

October 2022

Rajesh Singh
Valentina Emilia Balas
Arpan Kumar Kar
Anita Gehlot
Shahab Shamshirband

Organization

Chief Patron

Shri Jitendra Joshi   Uttaranchal University, India

Patrons

Satbir Sehgal   Uttaranchal University, India
Dharam Buddhi   Uttaranchal University, India
Rajesh Bahuguna   Uttaranchal University, India

Conference Chairs

Rajesh Singh   Uttaranchal University, India
Anita Gehlot   Uttaranchal University, India

Program Chairs

Valentina Emilia Balas   Aurel Vlaicu University of Arad, Romania
Arpan Kumar Kar   IIT Delhi, India
Shahab Shamshirband   National Yunlin University of Science and Technology, Taiwan

Conveners

Pradeep Suri   Uttaranchal University, India
Sonal Sharma   Uttaranchal University, India

Advisory Board

Onkar Singh   Uttarakhand Technical University, India
Rameshwar Dubey   Montpellier Business School, France
Constantin Blome   Lancaster University, UK
Julia Swart   Utrecht University, The Netherlands
Riktesh Srivastav   Skyline University, Sharjah, UAE
Mayank Singh   University of KwaZulu-Natal, South Africa
S. C. Sharma   IIT Roorkee, India
Durga Toshniwal   IIT Roorkee, India
Sonajharia Minz   JNU, India

Somil Kumar   Uttaranchal University, India
Neeti Misra   Uttaranchal University, India
Mukesh Pandey   Uttaranchal University, India
Pratibha Pandey   Uttaranchal University, India
Saurabh Pathak   Teerthanker Mahaveer University, India
Amarjeet Rawat   Uttaranchal University, India
Babita Rawat   Uttaranchal University, India
Vijaylakshmi Sajwan   Uttaranchal University, India
Ravindra Sharma   Swami Rama Himalayan University, India
Sameer Sharma   Uttaranchal University, India
Chandra Thukral   DIT, India

Organizing Committee

Rajiv Kumar   Uttaranchal University, India
Monisha Awasthi   Uttaranchal University, India
Sameer Dev Sharma   Uttaranchal University, India
Abhishek K. Pathak   Uttaranchal University, India
Amar Jeet Rawat   Uttaranchal University, India
Ishteyaaq Ahmed   Uttaranchal University, India
Vijay Laxmi Sajwan   Uttaranchal University, India
Praveen Shah   Uttaranchal University, India
Manisha Khanduja   Uttaranchal University, India
Vyshe   Uttaranchal University, India
Babita Rawat   Uttaranchal University, India
Deepa Bisht   Uttaranchal University, India
Deepti Sharma   Uttaranchal University, India
Rajeev Ranjan   Uttaranchal University, India
Anil Singh Chauhan   Uttaranchal University, India
B. C. Kandpal   Uttaranchal University, India
Rakesh Semwal   Uttaranchal University, India
Rohit Dhiman   Uttaranchal University, India
Sonakshi Bhatia   Uttaranchal University, India
Neeti Mishra   Uttaranchal University, India
Farman Ali   Uttaranchal University, India
Neha Rastogi   Uttaranchal University, India

Contents

Contents

Brain Stroke Prediction Using the Artificial Intelligence

Himani Maheshwari[1], Dharminder Yadav[2], and Umesh Chandra[3](✉)

[1] School of Computing, Graphic Era Hill University, Dehradun, Uttarakhand, India
himani_bahmah@yahoo.com
[2] Department of Computer Science and Technology, Glocal University, Saharanpur, UP, India
ydharminder@yahoo.com
[3] Department of Statistics and Computer Science, Banda University of Agriculture and
Technology, Banda, UP, India
uck.iitr@gmail.com

Abstract. The brain stroke was caused by the stress of the job and the quick pace
of life. The most frequent cause of morality in this time period is stroke. The
hazard of a brain stroke is greatly influenced by a number of variables, including
blood pressure, age, BMI, and hypertension. Stroke monitoring and prognosis
have received international interest due to the negative outcomes of stroke. To
correctly forecast the occurrence of stroke based on risk variables connected with
patients' electronic health records (EHRs), numerous data mining approaches
have been applied globally. EHRs frequently have thousands of attributes, the bulk
of which should be eliminated to increase prediction accuracy because they are
unnecessary or irrelevant. The selection of feature-extraction techniques can help
increase the model's predictive capability and facilitate effective data organization
of archived input characteristics. This research conducts a systematic analysis of
the different aspects in EHR records for stroke identification. In order to prioritize
the importance of various EHR records in precisely diagnosing strokes, we provide
a new, quite challenging technique. Using a variety of statistical approaches, we
recognize the features that are most important for stroke predictions. A perceptual
neural network with these four properties also offers the maximum accuracy rate
and minimum miss rate when measured against all accessible input features and
additional standardization procedures. We report our outcomes using a stable
dataset produced using sub-sampling methods because the sample is considerably
unbalanced in terms of the occurrence of strokes. Age, heart disease, glucose
level, smoking, and hypertension were found to be the most significant factors in
diagnosing stroke in patients when researchers tested the proposed technique on
a publicly available EHR dataset. We also contrasted the suggested method with
other well- liked feature-selection methods. To get the highest performance in
comparing the significance of individual features in the stroke detection technique
to other well-known feature-selection strategies, we employed machine learning
algorithms like random forest, KNN, etc. In order to rank the significance of
individual features in stroke detection, we employed machine learning algorithms
like random forest, KNN, etc.

Keywords: BMI · Machine leaning algorithm · Brain stroke · EHR · KNN · NN

R. Singh et al. (Eds.): ICBDA 2022, CCIS 1742, pp. 1–11, 2022.
https://doi.org/10.1007/978-3-031-23647-1_1

1   Introduction

Human existence is stressful and fast-paced today. Stroke is caused by stress, obesity, high blood pressure, and daily stress. A stroke is the second most prevalent cause of death [1]. A stroke is a condition in which the central nervous system does not receive enough blood flow, which causes cell death. Strokes can be either ischemic (loss of blood flow) or hemorrhagic (bleeding) [2]. One side of the body may experience trouble speaking or understanding, dizziness, or loss of vision as a result of a stroke. Strokes are mainly ischemic (around 87%) and hemorrhagic (the remaining 13%) [3]. Blood pressure(BP) is the biggest risk factor for stroke. Additional risk factors contain atrial fibrillation, BP, diabetes, obesity, and end-stage renal disease [4]. Human existence is stressful and fast-paced today. Stroke is caused by stress, obesity, high blood pressure, and daily stress. Around 87 percent of strokes are ischemic, while 13 percent are hemorrhagic [3]. Blood pressure is the biggest risk factor for stroke. Additional risk factors include end-stage renal disease, atrial fibrillation, high blood pressure, diabetes, smoking and obesity with a history of TIA [4].

17.7 million people died from cardiovascular diseases in 2017, with 6.7 million of those deaths attributable to stroke, according to the WHO [5]. The frequency of strokes and their mortality rates continue to climb [6]. On World Stroke Day each year, people are informed about stroke and its preventative measures [7]. To lessen the negative effects of stroke, early detection and prevention are crucial. The field of medical sciences has advanced significantly as a result of continual technological advancements [8]. A neurological examination, CT or MRI scans, Doppler ultrasonography, and arteriography are a few of the methods used to diagnose stroke. Clinical stroke diagnosis is made using imaging methods. The subtypes and causes of stroke can be identified with the help of imaging techniques. To identify risk factors and rule out other potential causes, additional investigations are carried out, such as blood tests and electrocardiograms (ECGs) [2]. Researchers have sought to use data mining as a replacement for radiography and other labor-intensive and expensive clinical diagnostic procedures to identify strokes.

Researchers can use data-mining techniques to find patterns in the data because annotated databases of medical records are now accessible. For medical professionals, such studies have made it simpler to give accurate prognoses for a variety of illnesses. The results are improved healthcare environments and lower treatment expenses. The use of data mining techniques to medical records has had a considerable impression on the domain of healthcare and biomedicine [9, 10]. This makes it possible for medical professionals to spot the disease's onset at an early stage. Finding the main causes of stroke and its contributing factors are of special interest to us. The collection of medical data has become easier thanks to the Internet of Things (IoT) as low-cost wearable devices are now readily available [11–13]. A significant amount of fundamental clinical data is gathered from these devices using various data-mining algorithms in order to find important trends. Additionally, the gathered data are used to make decisions in the healthcare sector and have proven to be a cost-saving element [14]. The study of health care sciences has developed into a strong machine learning industry in recent years (ML). To properly predict each patient's risk of having a stroke, EHRs and ML models can be employed [15]. How predictively accurate the forecasts are depending on the variables taken from the data. The forecasting model should only contain relevant results-related attributes in order to miximize the predicted accuracy of the training models and decrease the time needed for machine learning [16]. A number of data mining techniques have also been introduced [17–19] in order to pinpoint the essential and applicable data for predicting the incidence of strokes.

The main characteristics of this study includes a comprehensive understanding of the numerous risk factors for stroke prediction. An examination of the different components of patient Electronic Health Record (EHR) records to ascertain which components are most essential for stroke prediction. The effectiveness of well-known machine learning models for stroke prediction using a publically available dataset is compared. The dimensionality reduction method is used to discover patterns in the smallest sub-space of the feature space. All of the simulations included in this essay have online sources since we follow the rules of reproducible research.

2 Literature Review

Scientists are focusing on methods to prevent this issue and find an effective therapy due to the expanding number of patients with heart disease and the high costs associated with treating it. Several concepts have been put forth about the automated identification of heart stroke utilizing EHRs. Furthermore, accurate stroke risk assessment depends on selecting and recognizing the traits that influence a stroke's outcome [20]. A crucial clinical point that could lead to a decrease in the frequency of healthcare occurrences is the selection of the most crucial components from a much higher dimensional EHR. Numerous facets of stroke prognosis have been examined in earlier studies published in the literature. To estimate the likelihood of a stroke, Jeena et al. consider a number of risk variables [21]. A regression- based methodology was used to establish the connection between a trait and its impact on stroke. Hanifa and Raja [22] employed radial based functions and regression models in a non-linear SVM to improve the accuracy for predicting cardiovascular risk. Operational, healthcare, lifestyle, and demographic risk factors were divided into these four categories for the study. In [23], Min et al. created a method for determining prospective risk factors for stroke. In order to predict stroke in patients, Singh and Choudhary in [24] applied the classification tree technique to the Cardiovascular Health Study (CHS) collection. A feed-forward multi-layer ANN model was used to research the prediction of strokes in [25]. Similar investigations into the creation of a system that can predict strokes based on patient data were carried out in [26–28]. Hung et al's [29] investigation of machine learning and deep learning methods for predicting strokes from a computerized database of medical claims. In addition to traditional stroke prediction methods, Li et al. in [30] employed machine-learning algorithms to predict thromboembolism and ischemic stroke in atrial fibrillation.

Zhang et al. [31] study racking based and weighting hybrids feature selection (WRHFS), an effective classification choosing method, to understand the chance of stroke. The study methodology selected nine crucial criteria for stroke diagnosis out of 28 factors based on sufficient data. The authors of a different study [32] identified critical risk factors for predicting heart-disease from a very huge number of structures using a cardiovascular functionality selection algorithm. The ranks are established using the residues graph methodology and the infinite latent feature selection(ILFS) method for feature selection. The experiment only used half of the 50 heart disease factors, yet the output of the model was still useful. Support vector machines(SVM) [33], decision trees [34], deep neural networks [35], and ensemble techniques [36] are examples of models that, when given the right data, have produced remarkably accurate classifications of stroke prediction. Major risk factors were used by the authors of [37] to evaluate the effectiveness of Bayesian networks for predicting post-stroke outcomes. This study used the information gain strategy to weed out unnecessary attributes. Another study's researchers [38] offered a different method for feature extraction that relied on the conservative mean measure. The SVM classifier was combined with the feature extraction technique to categorize the stroke result based on a shortened functionality.

3   Data Set and Methodology Used

An EHR, also referred to as an electronic medical record(EMC), is where a patient's data is kept (EMR). Licensed healthcare practitioners submit information about a person's clinical status into a structured, computer-readable database. Vital signs, pathology, and the outcomes of an examination are among the information contained in the records. With the wise use of EHR, the future of medical diagnostics is bright. In this study, electronic health information from a public data source called Kaggle were linked to the prediction of brain strokes. Electronic health records for 4981 individuals are included in the collections. It has one output feature and eleven incoming attributes. The controller output, which is a binary object, shows whether or not a person has had a stroke. Client identification, sex (S), age (A), whether or not the patient has high blood pressure (HP), whether or not the patient has cardiovascular disease (HD), relationship status (MA), profession type (P), residential type (RT), mean glucose level (AGL), body mass index(BMI), and smoking habits are the typically about 10 attribute values in EHR (SM). In terms of the frequency of stroke events, the dataset is exceedingly unrepresentative; the vast majority of the entries in the dataset refer to patients who did not experience a stroke. The patient identifying feature will not be included in the discussion of this work that follows.

When continuous elements are included into meaningful groupings, they become simpler to comprehend. Discretization is the process of converting continuous qualities into discrete features by establishing a sequence of consecutive intervals that cover the characteristic value range. To improve the dataset and make it simpler to interpret, we discretized the three characteristics—average glucose level, BMI, occupation, and age. Despite the benefits of data discretization, in order to draw meaningful conclusions, we must carefully select the range of intervals/levels based on our medical expertise. There is mounting evidence that age has a substantial impact on how stroke risk variables are distributed [39]. Although the risk of stroke grows with age, not only the elderly are at risk. A medical study found that strokes can happen to anyone, from infants to adults. Participants in the sample range in age from 10 to 80. In the section that follows, the efficacy of ten patient features in detecting stroke from electronic health records was examined for each of them.

4 Data Analysis

4981 patients' records are included in the data, and none of the values are null. Only 5% of participants in the data had a stroke, while 95% of people did not. It suggests the data is out of balance and the outcome is unacceptable. We first determined the accuracy of a machine learning model using imbalanced data, then we balanced the data using a method that was available, determined the model's accuracy, and compared it to earlier models. Age, BMI, hypertension, heart disease, being married or not, work type, residence type, and average blood glucose level are the ten features in the data that are most important. However, the majority of the data for smoking status is unclear, therefore we removed this row to improve result prediction. The dataset has a 48% male and a 52% female population, yet the majority of people are stroke-free, making up only 6% of the total population. The percentages of married and single people are 66% and 34, respectively. The most significant risk factor for brain and heart attacks is smoking, although in the dataset, 30% of individuals' status was unclear, and just 37% of respondents were interested in smoking. Since more than 30% of participants did not know whether they smoked or not, we had to eliminate this feature from consideration. But the researcher is unable to draw the right conclusions. Another element that affects the stroke prognosis is the nature of job. According to the data, the private sector employs 57% of all workers in today's world, compared to 13% who work for the government, 14% who are youngsters, and 16% who are self-employed. Figure 1 shows the data distribution for stroke by age, location, heart condition, hypertension, and marital status.

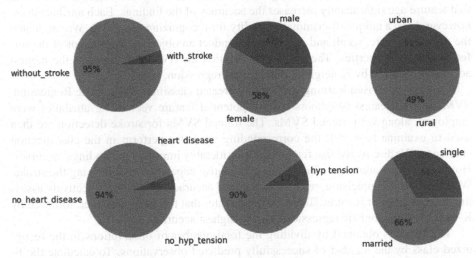

Fig. 1. Analysis of data distribution

The dataset contains age-specific data ranging from 0 to 80 years old, but the majority of the population in the data is male and female between the ages of 40 and 60. When the data on strokes in men and women were analyzed, it was discovered that the risk of stroke peaked between the ages of 60 and 80. Based on the statistics, we deduce that those between the ages of 50 and 80 also have a greater risk of developing heart disease.

But the 40 to 80 age range for hypertension is a significant determinant in the emergence of heart disease and stroke. BMI is applicable to both male and female as adults. The three categories under which BMI is classified are Underweight (18.5), Overweight (25- 29.9), Obesity BMI of 30 or greater, and Normal weight (18.5-24.9). Glycemia, sometimes called blood sugar or blood glucose, is the quantity of glucose in a person's blood. A 70 kg person's bloodstream contains about 4 grammes of glucose, a simple sugar, at all times [40].The dataset's unbalanced nature makes it challenging to create any machine learning models. We employed a stochastic down-sampling technique to lessen the detrimental effects of unequal data. The minority (248 observations) and the plurality were separated from the results (4733 observations). A balanced dataset is created with 248 observations from the majority and 248 from the minority. From a total of 4733 majority instances, we selected all 248 minority case facts and 248 random majority case insights. There are currently 496 observations in the balanced dataset. The symmetrical dataset was utilised for training 80% of the time and for performance evaluation 20% of the time.

5   Results and Discussion

We developed classifiers for Logistic Regression, SVM, and K-Nearest Neighbors using a supervised learning approach. Both trained SVMs and all ten candidate feature vectors for attributes were used. The performance of the corresponding characteristics in the classification task is next tested using the trained SVMs for stroke detection. We found that feature age significantly increases the accuracy of the findings. Each attribute does, however, have a unique discriminative ability for recognizing the stroke. We calculated the precision-score, recall and accuracy to conduct an objective assessment of the different dataset properties. The Table 1 shows that the SVM classifier has the highest accuracy, followed by K-neighbor and logistic regression.

Using a supervised learning strategy, we created classifiers for Logistic Regression, SVM, and K-Nearest Neighbors. All 10 potential feature vectors for attributes were employed, along with trained SVMs. The trained SVMs for stroke detection are then used to examine how well the corresponding attributes perform in the classification challenge. We discovered that feature age considerably improves the findings' accuracy. However, each feature has a distinct discriminative capacity for identifying the stroke. We calculated the precision, recall, F-score, and accuracy in order to objectively assess the different dataset features. Table 1 demonstrates that the SVM classifier, followed by K- neighbor and logistic regression, has the highest accuracy.

The recall is obtained by dividing the total number of observations in the recognized class by the number of successfully predicted observations. To calculate the F-Score, Recall and the harmonic mean of Precision is used. The proportion of precisely expected observations is the final definition of accuracy. The accuracy of the aforementioned method on the unbalanced data was unreliable, so we balanced the data using the "SMOTEENN" package. The data are unbalanced because there are 1373 patients without a stroke and 3318 patients with strokes, thus we added 4733 rows to restore equilibrium. The confusion matrix after the balancing data is shown in Table 2.

Table 1. Accuracy, precision, recall and F1-score of supervised algorithms

S. No	Name of classifier	Accuracy	Precision	Recall	F1-score
1	SVM	99.82	99	100	98
2	K-Neighbor	95	95	100	97
3	Logistic Regression	94.52	95	100	97
4	Random Forest	84	86	82	84

Table 2. Accuracy, Recall, F1-Score and Precision of supervised algorithms with balance data.

S. No	Classifier		Accuracy(%)	Precision(%)	Recall(%)	F1-score(%)
1	SVM	0	100	100	100	100
2		1		100	100	100
3	Logistic Regression		91	91	95	93

5.1 Model of Ensemble Voting

Various categorization models may be combined to create an ensemble model. We will use the Random Forest model, KNN, and Linear Regression to create an Ensemble Voting classifier. Linear Regression, KNN, and Random Forest are the three models in this Ensemble that each predict a different result from the training. Ensemble models exhibit lower error and overfitting when compared to individual models. Since every individual model has a distinct bias (or personality), the biases in the ensemble are averaged out. One of the ensemble approaches that combines the predictions of different models is the voting classifier. Soft voting, which averages the likelihood of predictions from numerous models, will be used. Because the accuracy of the ensemble model is worse than that of any other supervised algorithm—78.43%—we employed the XGBoost approach instead. One of the most potent ML algorithms currently being used is called Extreme Gradient Boosted Trees (XGBoost). We may also utilise regularization with XGBoost to avoid overfitting and produce a generic answer. The ensemble model XGBoost uses a number of decision trees as base learners. It resembles Random Forest. Additionally, we tried the well-liked XGBoost 72%, but it fell short of ensemble voting's 78% accuracy rate.

As most of the data were unknown and had little impact on stroke prediction, we removed the smoking status feature before running the supervised machine learning algorithm on the data. Balance the data 4733 rows with a stroke and 4733 rows without a stroke for a total of 9466 rows after the smoking status element has been removed. With an 80/20 split, separate the data into a train dataset and a test dataset. The training dataset has 7572 rows, whereas the testing dataset has 1894 rows. The random forest and decision tree's training and validation accuracy are shown in Table 3 respectively.

In predictive modelling, neural networks perform better because of the hidden layers. Input and output nodes are all that are needed by linear regression models to generate

Table 3. Training and validation accuracy, precision, recall and F1-score of Decision tree and random forest for balance data.

S. No	Classifier	Accuracy(%)		Precision(%)	Recall(%)	F1-score(%)
1	Decision Tree	Training	100	99	100	98
		Validation	95			
2	Random Forest	Training	99	94	100	97
		Validation	94			

forecasts. The neural network also makes advantage of the hidden layer to boost prediction precision. This is because it "learns" in a manner similar to how people do. The accuracy for training and validation was 94% after 300 cycles. Figure 2 displays the training and validation accuracy after 300 iterations.

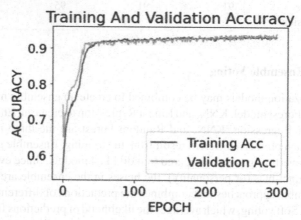

Fig. 2. Training and validation accuracy with epoch.

Two approaches are available in the randomised hyper parameter search tool, RandomizedSearchCV: "fit"and "score." Additionally, it implements "predict proba" , "decision function", "score samples", "predict", "inverse transform" and "transform" if the estimator supports them. The assessor assumptions necessary to implement these approaches are optimised through cross-validated search across hyperparameters. Instead of testing out every potential parameter value, like in GridSearchCV, a predetermined range of configurations are sampled from the specified populations. The n-iter specifies how many parameter settings will be tested. A sample without replacement operation will be carried out if a list of all the parameters is given. Sampling with auxiliary is utilised when at least 1 parameter is provided as a distribution. Consistent distributions should be utilised for continuous parameters. RandomizedSearchCV implemented using five cross validations, five estimators, and a depth of ten with a single increment. But compared to other algorithms, this technique did not attain the maximum accuracy. The method's accuracy is 79%, which is higher than XGBoost and Ensemble but lower than Neural Network and Supervised Machine Learning Algorithm.

6 Conclusion

This article presents an extensive investigation of patient factors in electronic health records for stroke diagnosis. Here, several characteristics were thoroughly explored. Through feature extraction and a step-by-step examination, the optimal set of characteristics was determined. It is discovered that the connections between the various attributes are weak, and that combining a variety of factors might greatly enhance stroke prediction. However, both the balancing data with and without a stroke have the same level of accuracy. In this study, decision trees, neural networks, SVM, and random forests were used. Random forest validation accuracy maintains at 94%, which is fairly good compared to XGBoost and n-ensemble approach, while decision tree validation accuracy increases to 95% after balancing the data neural network. The outcomes demonstrate that the dimension of the database has an impact on the outcome. Future stroke diagnoses will benefit from a machine-learning approach built on the characteristics identified in electronic health data. Additionally, the suggested rough-set technique may be applied in real-world application circumstances.

References

1. Pathan, M.S., Jianbiao, Z., John, D., Nag, A., Dev, S.: Identifying stroke indicators using rough sets. IEEE Access **8**, 210318–210327 (2020)
2. What Is a Stroke?. www.nhlbi.nih.gov/. March 26, 2014. Archived from the original on 18 February 2015. Retrieved 26 February 2015
3. Donnan, G.A., Fisher, M., Macleod, M., Davis, S.M.: Stroke. Lancet **371**(9624), 1612–1623 (2008). https://doi.org/10.1016/S0140-6736(08)60694-7
4. Hu, A., Niu, J., Winkelmayer, W.C.: Oral anticoagulation in patients with end-stage kidney disease on dialysis and atrial fibrillation. Semin. Nephrol. **38**(6), 618–628 (2018)
5. Shikany, J.M., et al.: 'Abstract P520: Associations of dietary patterns and risk of sudden cardiac death in the reasons for geographic and racial differences in stroke study differ by history of coronary heart disease. Circulation **141**(1), AP520 (2020)
6. Mourguet, M., et al.: Increased ischemic stroke, acute coronary artery disease and mortality in patients with granulomatosis with polyangiitis and microscopic polyangiitis. J. Autoimmunity **96**, 134–141 (2019)
7. Lindsay, M.P., et al.: World stroke organization (WSO): Global stroke fact sheet 2019. Int. J. Stroke **14**(8), 806–817 (2019)
8. Sivapalan G., Nundy K., Dev S., Cardiff B., Deepu J. ANNet: A lightweight neural network for ECG anomaly detection in IoT edge sensors IEEE Transactions on Biomedical Circuits and Systems (2) (2022)
9. Koh, H.C., Tan, G., et al.: Data mining applications in healthcare. J. Healthc. Inf. Manage. **19**(2), 65 (2011)
10. Yoo, I., et al.: Data mining in healthcare and biomedicine: a survey of the literature. J. Med. Syst. **36**(4), 2431–2448 (2012)
11. Gold, S.: Clinical concept value sets and interoperability in health data analytics. In: Proceedings AMIA Annual Symposium Proceedings, p. 480 (2018)

12. Ma, Y., Wang, Y., Yang, J., Miao, Y., Li, W.: Big health application system based on health internet of things and big data. IEEE Access 5, 7885–7897 (2017)
13. Mettler, M.: Blockchain technology in healthcare: the revolution starts here. In: Proceedings IEEE 18th International Conference E-Health Netw, Applications Services, pp. 1–3 (2016)
14. Yadav, P., Steinbach, M., Kumar, V., Simon, G.: Mining electronic health records (EHRs): a survey. ACM Comput. Surv. 50(6), 1–40 (2018)
15. Chen, M., Hao, Y., Hwang, K., Wang, L., Wang, L.: Disease prediction by machine learning over big data from healthcare communities. IEEE Access 5, 8869–8879 (2017)
16. Amin, M.S., Chiam, Y.K., Varathan, K.D.: Identification of significant features and data mining techniques in predicting heart disease. Telematics Informat. 36, 82–93 (2019)
17. Esfahani, H.A., Ghazanfari, M.: Cardiovascular disease detection using a new ensemble classifier. In: Proceedings IEEE 4th International Conference Knowledge- Based Engineering Innovation (KBEI), pp. 1011–1014 (2017)
18. Kolukisa, B., et al.: Evaluation of classification algorithms, linear discriminant analysis and a new hybrid feature selection methodology for the diagnosis of coronary artery disease. In: Proceedings IEEE International Conference Big Data, pp. 2232–2238 (2018)
19. Ratajczak, R., Crispim-Junior, C.F., Faure, E., Fervers, B., Tougne, L.: Automatic land cover reconstruction from historical aerial images: an evaluation of features extraction and classification algorithms. IEEE Trans. Image Process. 28(7), 3357–3371 (2019)
20. Azhar, M.A., Thomas, P.A.: Comparative review of feature selection and classification modeling. In: Proceedings International Conference Advances Computing, Communication Control, pp. 1–9 (2019)
21. Jeena, R.S., Kumar, S.: Stroke prediction using SVM. In: Proceedings International Conference on Control, Instrumentation, Communication and Computational Technologies (ICCICCT), pp. 600–602 (2016). http://dx.doi.org/https://doi.org/10.1109/ICCICCT.2016.7988020
22. Hanifa, S.-M., Raja-S, K.: Stroke risk prediction through non-linear support vector classification models. Int. J. Adv. Res. Comput. Sci. 1(3), 4753 (2010)
23. Min, S.N., Park, S.J., Kim, D.J., Subramaniyam, M., Lee, K.-S.: Development of an algorithm for stroke prediction: a national health insurance database study in Korea. Eur. Neurol. 79(3–4), 214–220 (2018)
24. Singh, M.S., Choudhary, P.: Stroke prediction using artificial intelligence. In: 2017 8th Annual Industrial Automationand Electromechanical Engineering Conference (IEMECON), IEEE, pp. 158–161 (2017)
25. Chantamit-O, P.: Prediction of stroke disease using deep learning model
26. Khosla, A., Cao, Y., Lin, C.C.-Y., Chiu, H.-K., Hu, J., Lee, H.: An integrated machine learning approach to stroke prediction. In: Proceedings of the 16th ACM SIGKDD International Conference on Knowledge Discovery and Data mining, pp. 183–192 (2010)
27. Hung, C.-Y., Lin, C.-H., Lan, T.-H., Peng, G.-S., Lee, C.-C.: Development of an intelligent decision support system for ischemic stroke risk assessment in a population-based electronic health record database. PLoS ONE 14(3), e0213007 (2019)
28. Teoh, D.: Towards stroke prediction using electronic health records. BMC Med. Inform. Decis. Mak. 18(1), 1–11 (2018)
29. Hung, C.-Y., Chen, W.-C., Lai, P.-T., Lin, C.-H., Lee, C.-C.: Comparing deep neural network and other machine learningalgorithms for stroke prediction in a large- scale population-based electronic medical claims database. In: 2017 39th Annual International Conference of the IEEE Engineering in Medicine and Biology Society (EMBC), IEEE, pp. 3110–3113 (2017)
30. Li, X., et al.: Integrated machine learning approaches for predicting ischemic stroke and thromboembolism in atrial fibrillation. In: AMIA Annual Symposium Proceedings, 2016, American Medical Informatics Association, p. 799 (2016)

31. Zhang, Y., Zhou, Y., Zhang, D., Song, W.: A stroke risk detection: Improving hybrid feature selection method. J. Med. Internet Res. **21**(4), e12437 (2019)
32. Le, H.M., Tran, T.D., Tran, L.V.: Automatic heart disease prediction using feature selection and data mining technique. J. Comput. Sci. Cybern. **34**(1), 33–48 (2018)
33. Ayushi, D., Nikita, B., Nitin, S.: A survey of ECG classification for arrhythmia diagnoses using SVM. In:Intelligent Communication Technologies and Virtual Mobile Networks. Cham, Switzerland: Springer, 2019, pp. 574– 590. https://doi.org/10.1007/978-3-030-28364-3_59
34. Bin, G., Shao, M., Bin, G., Huang, J., Zheng, D., Wu, S.: Detection of atrial fibrillation using decision tree ensemble. In: Proceedings Computational Cardiology Conference, pp. 1–4 (2017)
35. Panwar, M., et al.: Rehab-net: deep learning framework for arm movement classification using wearable sensors for stroke rehabilitation. IEEE Trans. Biomed. Eng. **66**(11), 3026–3037 (2019)
36. Kavanagh, K., Roper, M., Young, D., Schraag, S.: Evaluation of random forest and ensemble methods at predicting complications following cardiac surgery. In: Artificial Intelligence in Medicine. AIME (Lecture Notes in Computer Science), vol. 11526, Riaño, D., Wilk, S., ten Teije, A., Eds.: Cham, Switzerland: Springer, p. 376 (2019). https://doi.org/10.100 7/978-3-030-21642-9_48
37. Park, E., Chang, H.-J., Nam, H.S.: A Bayesian network model for predicting post-stroke outcomes with available risk factors. Frontiers Neurol. **9**, 699 (2018)
38. Khosla, A., Cao, Y., Lin, C.C.-Y., Chiu, H.-K., Hu, J., Lee, H.: An integrated machine learning approach to stroke prediction. In: Proceedings 16th ACM SIGKDD International Conference Knowledge Discovery Data Mining, pp. 183–192 (2010)
39. Kelly-Hayes, M.: Influence of age and health behaviors on stroke risk: lessons from longitudinal studies. J. Amer. Geriatrics Soc. **58**, S325–S328 (2010)
40. Wasserman, D.H.: Four grams of glucose. American J. Physiology. Endocrinology and Metabolism. **296**(1), E11–21 (2009)

Game Rules Prediction – Winning Strategies Using Decision Tree Algorithms

A. Mansurali[1]([✉]) [ID], V. Harish[2] [ID], Sherin Hussain[1] [ID], and Ravindra Sharma[3] [ID]

[1] School of Business and Management, Christ University, Bangalore, India
mansurali.a@christuniversity.in
[2] PSG Institute of Management PSG College of Technology, Coimbatore, India
[3] Himalayan School of Management Studies, Swami Rama Himalayan University, Dehradun, India

Abstract. With the availability of extensive data spanning over the years, sports have become an emerging field of research. The application of analytics in cricket has become prominent over the years. Cricket, the most loved sport in India, draws the attention of fans worldwide. The Indian Premier League is no exception. Created in 2008, this franchise-based T20 format of cricket has gripped the attention of cricket enthusiasts. With ardent fans cheering for their favorite teams, teams have mounting pressure to maintain their winning streak. One such team is the beloved Chennai Super Kings. Statistical techniques for winner prediction have become popular over the last decade. In this study, we try to frame decision rules for IPL teams to win a series using the CART algorithm. By considering Chennai Super Kings, this study aims to understand the criteria for winning and identify potential weaknesses, allowing the team to predict the likelihood of winning the IPL series.

Keywords: Sport · Indian Premiere League · Batsman · Clustering · Profiling

1 Introduction

Analytics, data science, and big data are some of the terms that have become prominent in recent years. It has applications across sectors such as banking and healthcare, most notably in the rapidly growing area such as sports. The explosion of data and the availability of datasets for analysis has impacted every aspect of life. Extensively available data sources have driven this impact, the advent of new technologies, and advances in machine learning, enabling better real-time insights (Ishi & Patil, 2021). Data-driven decision-making has become a norm, and the sports industry is no exception (Jayal et al. 2018). Sports is a growing business, as indicated by the valuation of major professional sports teams in USA and across the world (Miller, 2016).Sports is an ideal domain for exploring research areas since data from numerous sporting events spanning many years is readily available to the public (Fry & Ohlmann, 2012). Over the last decade, statistics in sports have proliferated and changed how strategies have been formed, and players are evaluated.

© The Author(s), under exclusive license to Springer Nature Switzerland AG 2022
R. Singh et al. (Eds.): ICBDA 2022, CCIS 1742, pp. 12–23, 2022.
https://doi.org/10.1007/978-3-031-23647-1_2

The two main types of sports data-driven analysis are on-field and off-field approaches. The sports industry, both on the field and the business side, uses data to gain an edge over competitors.

Cricket is a recognized sport which is played and watched across the world in over 100 countries (Vistro et al. 2019). Cricket is a beloved sport in India which has evolved over the years. Cricket is currently being played in three formats: ODIs, Test Matches and T20 (Shah, 2017). The T20 format is the latest and has quickly become the most exciting format for cricket fans. Created in 2008, the Indian Premier League has had over ten seasons and is one of the finest twenty-20 cricketing series in the world (Tekade et al. 2020).

The likelihood of winning a match can be predicted to a certain extent by factors such as player performance, toss, venue, and so on. The regression analysis has shown that other factors, such as weather, lighting, and pitch condition, could impact the match's outcome (Dawson et al. 2009). By implementing ML algorithms, players' performance in upcoming matches can be predicted. By predicting future performance, it is possible to ensure better team selection (Anik et al. 2018). Several attributes of the game can determine the result of a match. Toss, run rate, remaining wickets, and strike-rate are some examples of in-game attributes. Pre-game details include match venue, innings, records etc. Decision Trees have been used here to analyze these attributes' effect on a match's result. Over the last decade, statistical techniques, especially for winner prediction, have become increasingly popular.

2 Literature Review

Winner prediction has become a topic of interest, especially for T20 matches. Projections can be made before the start of the game or while the match is ongoing (Yasir et al. 2017). Several research studies have been done on predicting the outcome of a match. Kampakis and Thomas used a dataset comprising 2009 to 2014 data of the English-twenty over county cricket cup to propose a machine learning model. The model used features such as strike rate, home team and away team. The model evaluated these features to predict the outcome of a match (Kampakis & Thomas, 2015).

Both the score of a match and the winning team can be predicted, for predicting the score of a match, linear regression, lasso regression, and ridge regression can be used and SVC, decision tree, and random forest classifier are used to predict the winning team (Basit et al. 2020).

The study conducted by Chowdhury uses logistic regression to calculate match outcome probabilities and to determine the impact of the Indian team's match victories based on the toss, home-field advantage, day or night play, and choice of first batting (Chowdhury et al. 2020).

The impact on the probability of winning a match due to the toss and batting order can be determined using Logit regression models. The findings suggested that batting first and winning the toss increased the probability of winning a match (Dawson et al. 2009).

Factors such as day and night effect, toss, and home advantage are examples of some factors which can be analyzed using ML algorithms, namely Bayesian classifiers, to predict how these factors can affect the outcome of an ODI match (Kaluarachchi & Varde, 2010).

A prediction model using logistic regression and k-means was used to predict the outcome of ODI matches (Naik et al. 2018).

By using ML algorithms such as KNN, Logistic Regression, Random Forest, and decision tree, Jhanwar et al. could predict the winner of ODI matches with an accuracy of 71% (Jhanwar & Pudi 2016).

Daniel et al. proposed that even before a match begins, the winner can be predicted by algorithms like Naïve Bayes, SVM, Random Forest, Decision Tree, and Logistic Regression, and this can help in determining the strengths of the team (Vistro et al. 2019).

Agrawal et al. 2018 have previously tried to study the problems encountered when trying to predict which team will win an IPL match. The study focused on the competency of players individually, aspects such as teamwork and coordination, and the technique utilized by the teams in a match, and tried to predict which team would win based on historical data by applying ML algorithms like SVM and Naive Bayes (Agrawal et al. 2018).

Dynamic winner prediction has been addressed in a study by identifying features such as the relative strength of teams. By using supervised learning algorithms such as Random Forest Classifier, the winning team can be predicted based on the composition of the competing team (Viswanadha et al. 2017).

Khan et al. considered factors such as toss outcome, venue, teams competing, etc., to apply supervised learning techniques such as Naïve Bayes and SVM for predictive analysis in ODI matches (Khan et al. 2019).

Deep C Prakash, C Patwardhan et al. presented a Deep Mayo Predictor model, which was used to predict the winner of the ninth season of the Indian Premier League. The match outcome was predicted based on modeling the strengths of the players (Deep et al. 2016).

Yasir et al. proposed a winner prediction technique that used factors such as the history of the player, weather conditions, and winning percentage.

A model was proposed by RameshwariLokhande and P.M. Chawan, which could predict the outcome of an ongoing match. This could be done by selecting features such as the number of fallen wickets, the ranking of the teams, pitch status and the venue of the match (Lokhande & Chawan 2018).

The study conducted by Jayalath et al. uses CART and the logistic approach to quantify the significance of the possible predictors, such as home advantage, toss result, day or day and night match, and bat first or second, and thereby predict the outcome of the match (Jayalath 2018).

3 Methodology

The research follows an exploratory design to achieve its objective, as the technique employed will generate the winning rules for the cricket team. A supervised learning method was applied to the dataset as both the input variables and target variable is known in this case. Decision Tree algorithm, supervised learning method has been employed in

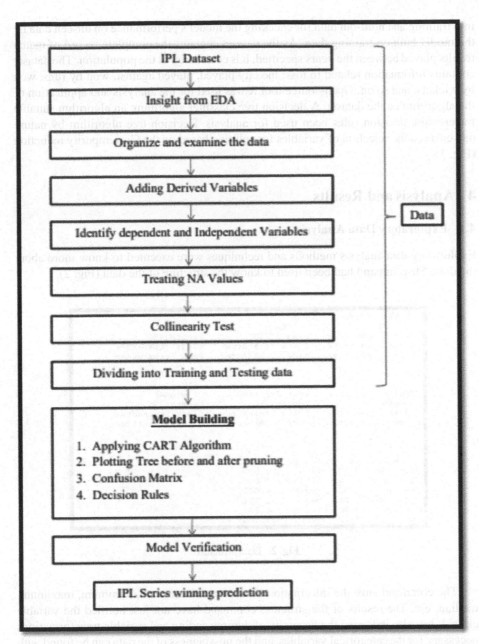

Fig. 1. Methodology- flow chart

the process of finding the results as the dataset had more number of categorical variables. Secondary data collection method had been adopted for the data collection. Data had been extracted from the secondary source ESPN Cricinfo. The data contains 756 data points; the IPL matches played from the year 2007 to 2019 with 19 variables. Data had been split into training and hold-out data for checking the model's performance on unseen data by the model built on training data. As the dataset contains the complete record of match results played between the years specified, it is considered as the population. The dataset contains information related to toss; the city played, played against, won by runs, won by wickets, and so on. Open-source tool R was used for the analysis and application of the algorithm on the dataset. A decision tree classifier algorithm, an algorithm suitable for creating decision rules been used for analysis. Decision tree algorithm by nature had ensured the selection of variables for splitting based on the Gini impurity reduction (Fig. 1).

4   Analysis and Results

4.1   Exploratory Data Analysis

Exploratory data analysis methods and techniques were executed to know more about the data. Str command had been used to know the structure of the data (Fig. 2).

```
> summary(Team)
     city                   team1                   team2
Length:756              Length:756              Length:756
Class :character        Class :character        Class :character
Mode  :character        Mode  :character        Mode  :character


  toss_winner            toss_decision             winner
Length:756              Length:756              Length:756
Class :character        Class :character        Class :character
Mode  :character        Mode  :character        Mode  :character


  win_by_runs          win_by_wickets
Min.   :   0.00      Min.   : 0.000
1st Qu.:   0.00      1st Qu.: 0.000
Median :   0.00      Median : 4.000
Mean   :  13.28      Mean   : 3.351
3rd Qu.:  19.00      3rd Qu.: 6.000
Max.   : 146.00      Max.   :10.000
```

Fig. 2. Data structure

The command gave the information about the variable class, minimum, maximum, median, etc. The results of the structure command have not just notified the variable class. It has also indicated the necessity of dummy coding and variable transformations necessary for the categorical variables, and the missingness of the data can be found with the same command using the values of NA. But the dataset doesn't have any missing values, which have been confirmed with the help of Fig. 2 above, as there are no NAs could be seen in the output.

Visualizing the Data
A basic visualization plot Histogram had been plotted on two data points, such as win by runs and won by wickets, and represented in the figures below.

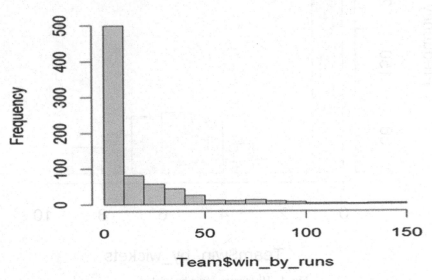

Fig. 3. Histogram – win by runs

The histogram in Fig. 3 above clearly indicates that the win by runs is right-skewed, which also reveals the data points are most cluttered towards the left side; that win by runs is always less. The same pattern is revealing the nature of this short format cricket that the majority of winning margins are very low, and to specify, it's less than ten the majority of the time. It also notifies that the data point is normally distributed, which needs to be treated in model-building exercises if required. The decision tree algorithm automatically categorizes the win by runs to less than and greater in the process. But with respect to the histogram of a win by wickets, close to normality is observed in the data, as in Fig. 4 below.

Histogram of Team$win_by_wickets

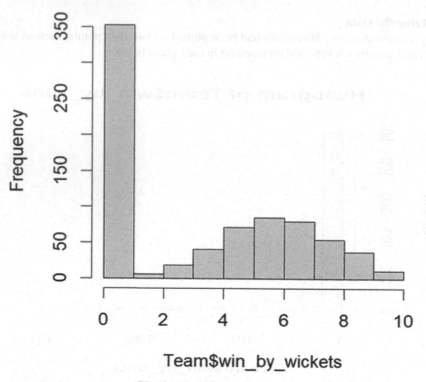

Fig. 4. Histogram – win by wickets

With respect to the number of wins by wickets, it really varies a lot to the team who wins in the IPL. From Fig. 4, it's obvious that the matches have been won by wickets ranging from 0 to 10, and there is a considerable number of wins also in each bucket. That shows the dominance of the batter and the necessity of power-hitting in a format like IPL, where the match can be won by a few players' great innings and pushing the team to win by wickets in different ranges. And is also, in IPL, it is clear that the maximum number of wins is in the range of fewer wickets, indicating that the IPL is a format of cricket that can be won with the help of the last men in the team, who are bowlers largely.

Decision Tree

CART algorithm had been deployed to frame a set of rules for the teams to win the series based on past data. Decision rules for IPL teams to win the series is an outcome attempted by this research, and the Chennai Super Kings team's winning information, such as win and loss of the match, has been considered as a target variable. The CART algorithm starts at the root node and splits from the child node to a terminal node based on the GINI index. At every step, the CART algorithm reduces the impurity of misclassification, leading to the classification with the maximum purity achieved compared to the root node. Rpart- Recursive partitioning and regression algorithm had been used to create the decision tree with its tuning parameters such as cp, minsplit, and xval (Fig. 6).

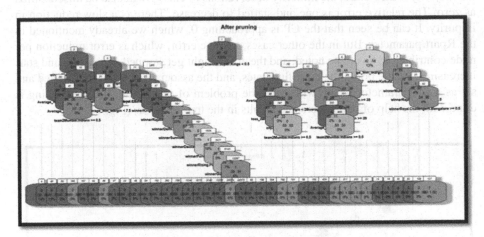

Fig. 5. Decision Tree Before Pruning

The above is the graphical output of the decision tree model developed on the training dataset. To explain the diagram (Fig. 5), for example, in Node 1, 93 percent of the observations are 0 class, and it's been marked as zero. The first variable taken to split is played against, followed by the margin of runs. Since the tree is grown too long, it will have the problem of overfitting, and it may not work well on unseen data. To overcome the problem of overfitting and to work well on the unseen data, there are two ways to avoid it, one using cross-validation, and the other method is pruning the tree, which is merging back the nodes.

```
Root node error: 79/600 = 0.13167

n= 600

          CP nsplit rel error  xerror     xstd
1 0.1645570      0  1.000000 1.00000 0.104841
2 0.1139241      1  0.835443 0.96203 0.103126
3 0.0253165      3  0.607595 0.70886 0.090197
4 0.0189873     16  0.202532 0.54430 0.079976
5 0.0126582     20  0.113924 0.34177 0.064277
6 0.0063291     24  0.063291 0.30380 0.060759
7 0.0042194     28  0.037975 0.30380 0.060759
8 0.0001000     37  0.000000 0.35443 0.065399
```

Fig. 6. Error and CP

And it can be seen that the root node error is 0.13167 because, at the root node, there are 79 observations of class 1 existing out of the total observations, which is 600. Being the majority is zero class; the minority observations of class 1 will also be misclassified as zero. The relative error is one and started to decrease. There is a slow reduction in impurity. It can be seen that the CP is approaching 0, which we already mentioned in the Rpart parameter. But in the other cases, relative error, which is error reduction per node contribution, has to be noted, and the error might get stopped decreasing and start increasing. So, the point, the error fluctuates, and the associated CP has to be noted and set as a CP parameter which will avoid the problem of overfitting. So, the pruning is done with the help of parameters and results in the tree as below (Fig. 7)

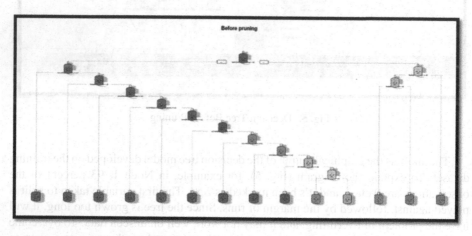
Before pruning

Fig. 7. Decision Tree After pruning

With the pruned model, the prediction was made on the hold-out dataset, and the results are as follows with an accuracy of 94% (Fig. 8).

```
> with (Team.holdout, table(winnerchennai.super.kings, predic
t.class))
                         predict.class
winnerchennai.super.kings   0    1
                     0  128    7
                     1    2   19
```

Fig. 8. Confusion matrix

The ultimate goal of the decision tree is to generate rules for the business and in this case, to win the match for CSK is to win the toss, the team against is Mumbai Indians and to have 30 runs more than the average, and to ensure two wickets difference.

5 Managerial Applications

- Understanding the criteria which lead to wins for a team helps to build strategies to maximize winnings.
- From a business perspective, this helps maximize earnings for a franchise team.
- Areas of weaknesses can be identified for a team from the decision rules
- Weakness of the team and improve the likelihood of winning measures can be taken with the help of decision rules
- By using CART, the probability of winning an IPL series can be identified, and this is useful in knowing the likelihood of a team's performance in an IPL series.

6 Methodological Limitations

- Time-consuming when the inputs increase, leading to training time complexity
- Overfitting is a major issue that needs to be solved by setting constraints on the parameters model and pruning method.
- Overfitting leads to high variance in the output leading to errors
- As decision tree is a nonparametric technique, it's not recommended to make generalizations based on results observed
- Considers even noisy data and trying to fit the data leading to the generation of new nodes, thereby making the tree too complex to interpret
- The addition of new data points leads to a recalculation of nodes to regenerate the overall tree.
- Change in the dataset makes the tree structure unstable, which causes variance.

7 Conclusion

Sports is a domain in the history which uses data, techniques, analytics and methods to increase its efficiency. With respect to the sports industry, cricket is the game which has celebrated widely and the game had proven history big time revenue generation model. Indian Premier League, the world's biggest league in term of viewers and revenue next to football had changed the whole gamut of game. IPL, the short format cricket attracted many businesses and players has also used data and techniques extensively and there is still larger scope of analytics for prediction of players selection, winning rules and so. Thus, this paper attempted to create such winning rules for the team with the previous data using supervised learning algorithm like decision tree. The main objective is to frame decision rules for IPL teams to win the series using the CART algorithm. The CART algorithm can be deployed based on past data to frame a set of rules for the IPL teams to win the series. From a business perspective, it is highly useful to understand the criteria on which a team wins an IPL series. By using the Decision Tree Algorithm, we can predict the probability of a team winning the IPL series. This is especially useful in knowing the likelihood of a team's performance in the IPL series, along with the winning rules. The major outcome of any tree is decision rules which helps to classify has helped here in the case of winning rules for classifying the matches into win or lose eventually helping the team, franchisors and coach.

References

Agrawal, S., Singh, S.P., Sharma, J.K.: Predicting results of Indian Premier League T-20 matches using machine learning. In: 2018 8th International Conference on Communication Systems and Network Technologies (CSNT) (2018)

Anik, A.I., Yeaser, S., Hossain, A.G., Chakrabarty, A.: Player's performance prediction in ODI cricket using machine learning algorithms. In: 2018 4th International Conference on Electrical Engineering and Information & Communication Technology (iCEEiCT) (2018)

Basit, A., Alvi, M.B., Jaskani, F.H., Alvi, M., Memon, K.H., Shah, R.A.: ICC T20 Cricket World Cup 2020 winner prediction using machine learning techniques. In: 2020 IEEE 23rd International Multitopic Conference (INMIC) (2020)

Chowdhury, S., Islam, K.M., Rahman, M.D.M., Raisa, T.S., Zayed, N.M.: One day International (ODI) cricket match prediction in logistic analysis: India vs. Pakistan. Int. J. Hum. Mov. Sports Sci. 8, 543–548 (2020)

Dawson, P., Morley, B., Paton, D., Thomas, D.: To bat or not to bat: an examination of match outcomes in day-night limited overs cricket. J. Oper. Res. Soc. 60, 1786–1793 (2009)

Deep, C., Patvardhan, C., Vasantha, C.: Data analytics based deep mayo predictor for IPL-9. Int. J. Comput. Appl. 152, 6–11 (2016)

Fry, M.J., Ohlmann, J.W.: Introduction to the special issue on analytics in sports, part I: general sports applications. Interfaces 42, 105–108 (2012)

Ishi, M.S., Patil, J.B.: A study on machine learning methods used for team formation and winner prediction in cricket. In: Smys, S., Balas, V.E., Kamel, K.A., Lafata, P. (eds.) Inventive Computation and Information Technologies. LNNS, vol. 173, pp. 143–156. Springer, Singapore (2021). https://doi.org/10.1007/978-981-33-4305-4_12

Jayal, A., McRobert, A., Oatley, G., O'Donoghue, P.: Sports Analytics Analysis, Visualisation and Decision Making in Sports Performance. Routledge Taylor & Francis Group, London (2018)

Jayalath, K.P.: A machine learning approach to analyze ODI cricket predictors. J. Sports Analytics 4, 73–84 (2018)

Jhanwar, M.G., Pudi, V.: Predicting the outcome of ODI cricket matches: a team composition based approach. In: ECML (2016)

Kaluarachchi, A., Varde, A.S.: CricAI: a classification based tool to predict the outcome in ODI cricket. In: 2010 Fifth International Conference on Information and Automation for Sustainability (2010)

Kampakis, S., Thomas, W.: Using machine learning to predict the outcome of english county twenty over cricket matches. arXiv: Machine Learning (2015)

Khan, J.R., Biswas, R.K., Kabir, E.: A quantitative approach to influential factors in one day international cricket: analysis based on Bangladesh. J. Sports Analytics 5, 57–63 (2019)

Lokhande, R., Chawan, P.M.: Live cricket score and winning prediction. Int. J. Trend Res. Dev. 5 (2018)

Miller, T.W.: Sports Analytics and Data Science: Winning the Game with Methods and Models. Pearson Education Inc, Old Tappan, NJ (2016)

Naik, A., Pawar, S., Naik, M., Mulani, S.: Winning prediction analysis in One-Day-International (ODI) cricket using machine learning techniques. Int. J. Emerg. Technol. Comput. Sci. 3, 137–144 (2018)

Shah, P.: Predicting outcome of live cricket match using duckworth- Lewis Par score. Int. J. Syst. Sci. Appl. Math. 2, 83 (2017)

Tekade, P., Markad, K., Amage, A., Natekar, B.: Cricket match outcome prediction using machine learning. Int. J. Adv. Sci. Res. Eng. Trends 5 (2020)

Vistro, D.M., Rasheed, F., David, L.G.: The cricket winner prediction with application of machine learning and data analytics. Int. J. Sci. Technol. Res. 8 (2019)

Viswanadha, S., Sivalenka, K., Jhawar, M.G., Pudi, V.: Dynamic winner prediction in Twenty20 Cricket: based on relative team strengths. In: ECML (2017)

Yasir, M., Chen, L.I., Shah, S.A., Akbar, K., Sarwar, M.U.: Ongoing match prediction in T20 International. Int. J. Comput. Sci. Netw. Secur. **17**, 176–181 (2017)

Quantitative Analysis of the Impact of Demography and Job Profile on the Organizational Commitment of the Faculty Members in the HEI'S of Uttarakhand

Amit Kumar Uniyal[1](✉), Pooja Kanojia[1], Rupa Khanna[1], and Anil Kumar Dixit[2]

[1] Graphic Era Deemed to be University, Dehradun, India
amituniyal171@gmail.com
[2] Uttaranchal University, Dehradun, India

Abstract. Attainment, growth and prosperity of any education institute are dependent on the faithfulness, zealous, purposeful faculty involved in research and academics. Faculty is the performers and has different roles in the study hall and the entire community. Their involvement contributes in the enhancement of skills, ability, knowledge, innovation, creativity and frame of mind of the entire community. For a long time the construct Organizational commitment has been the area of interest. Organizational commitment is a very complicated and a complex matter. The issue of committed faculty is becoming a blatant discouragement and lacuna. To meliorate this issue the research intend to explore the effects of demographic profile like age, gender, marital status, education, place on OC of the teaching staff working in the HEI's of Uttarakhand.

Keywords: Affective · Continuance · Normative · Commitment

1 Introduction

Notion of organizational commitment has developed and grown in the literature on organizational and industrial psychology. Organizational commitment has gained ample and extensive importance and interest to try to know and attempt to bring out the clarity on the dedication and commitment of an employee. Numerous scholars have attempted to look into how organizational commitment affects employee motivation. (Mathieu & Zajac, 1990) and on the attendance of the employees (Meyer & Allen 1997). Employee emotional investment in the organization can be considered as Organisational commitment. To which he is associated with. Organizational commitment is the attitude related to work (Porter, Steers, et al. 1974).Attitude of an employee influence the conduct towards situation, individuals, group of people, in a way that helps in strengthening the employee's relationship within the organization (Buchanan, 1974).

The primary duty in the development of the nation is performed by the higher education institutions of the nation by providing quality education. Regards to this it's relevant to say that educational institutes should productively make use of the resources for the said development. For the same purpose a pool of dedicated and committed faculty is required (Shah, Fakhr, et al. 2010). For sustainable education system in the higher education system organizational commitment is the foundation. For the success of the higher education institutes organizational commitment is the most important factor (Bhatnagar, 2007). Higher education institutes yields highly skilled and professionals who can bring a positive change in every sphere only through the dedication of the faculty engaged with them. Excellence in the education can only be accomplished if the faculty is performing. This can only be ascertained if the faculty engaged in the organization is satisfied from the culture, policies and norms of the organization. In the private sector the demand for talented, professional and highly skilled faculty is increasing. Such candidate are offered good pay package by such universities. Higher education institutions face issues in sustaining such employees for a brief period of time (Suki, 2011).Thus the entire profile of the institutes can be affected by faculty who are deeply connected with their institutes.

2 Literature Review

A Iqbal, Kokash, et al. (2011) in their study He made an effort to determine how demographic factors affected the faculty members' organisational commitment. Working In the Saudi Arabian Kingdom University. High-achieving employees in terms of education have les commitment towards their organization. It was also revealed employees with high tenure in the same organization have high level of commitment.

Yucel and Bektas (2012) He explored on the connection between organisational commitment (OC) and teacher satisfaction. He also wanted to explore and moderate the age of the teacher with OC and job contentment in Turkey. Its target was secondary schools. It was revealed that younger teachers are more emotionally attached with the organization whereas older teachers have moderate level of commitment with the organization they are associated with.

Elkhdr and Kanbur (2018) tries to perceive the organizational commitment level amongst the teachers working at Libyan University differentiated amongst their gender, marital status, age, designation and status of the university. It was observed that marital status effect the organizational commitment. Married people are more committed towards their organization, also organizational commitment is high when the employee is older in an organization and the tenure of an employee is also positively related with the organizational commitment (O.C.)

Viet (2015) explored the demographic considerations on the O.C. of university lectures. Convenient sampling method was used. It was discovered that there was little association between academic tenure and continued dedication of the faculty working in the university, affective commitment and tenure of the faculty in the organization, normative commitment and the level of education of the faculty. There was moderate level of commitment between affective commitment and the designation of the faculty. Age and normative commitment are negatively correlated.

Gopinath (2020) The study was carried out in Tamil Nadu. Data were gathered using a stratified purposive random sampling technique. The study's goal was to determine how age, gender, educational level, designation, and years of experience affected certain outcomes pertaining to the organization's commitment, involvement, and job satisfaction. It was revealed that age, years of experience, education and gender have no significant difference between faculty and OC job involvement and job satisfaction.

Bashir and Gani (2020) focused on knowing the level of O.C. among the faculty in the higher education also in determining the factors that affect the teachers' organisational commitment, as well as to assess how different teachers' perspectives are based on various demographic parameters. It was revealed that male employees value nature of the job and rewards therefore they can change the job frequently, unmarried faculty have the highest level of commitment, teachers below the age of 40 do not wish to leave the job as they possess less work experience.

Tandon, Mishra, et al. (2020) explores the relationship between the demographic profile and the employee commitment amongst the workers in the service industry of India. Study was conducted in the private universities, structures questionnaire as a tool was utilized for collecting primary data. The research stated that while marital status and gender of the employees had no significant effect on the employees' degree of dedication, experience and age of the employees have a substantial impact.

Agrawal & Jain (2020) He looked into how the demographics affected the dedication of the school teachers. The study was conducted in Nepal. The sample size was 232 school teachers from Kathmandu. It was revealed in the study that education level and gender of the teachers do not differ for affective, normative and continuance commitment. It was revealed in the study that affective commitment is enhanced as the employee spends more time in an organization.

Govindaraju (2018) triesto find out the effect of demographic factors on the employee retention. It was revealed that employee with low turnover intention have highest tenure in the organization, there exist a favorable relationship between the education of the employees and the turnover intention. Also there exists a positive relationship between employee gender and employee retention.

Sandhu and Kapoor (2017) investigated how age and gender affected the teachers' organisational commitment. Data were gathered using a random sampling technique. The study was conducted in Dayalbagh education institutes of Agra in Uttar Pradesh. It was shown that when it comes to organisational dedication, there are no appreciable differences between men and women. It was also observed in the study marital status also has no significant difference with respect to organizational commitment.

Yadav & Srivasatava (2021) investigated how demographic factors affected organisational commitment in the education sector of India. The study examined how gender, age, marital status, and years of experience affected the organisational commitment of the private university's teachers. It was seen that there is a sizable distinction amongst employee's engagement between unmarried and married people. Age and teaching experience have no discernible effects on organisational commitment.

3   Research Methodology

As per the demand of the study both primary and secondary data are included. Primary information was collected with the aid of online Google forms. A questionnaire for the constructs- Affective, Continuance, and Normative was adapted from Allen and Mayers. There were 24 questions out of which 17 were positively keyed and 9 were negatively keyed. A 5-point Likert scale was adopted. Out of the total organizations targeted there were about 26 colleges and Universities from Dehradun, Haridwar, Rishikesh. Excel and SPSSS- AMOS were used for data analysis. Leavens test cannot be done in Excel.

Test for reliability of the internal scale: Cronbach Alpha for Affective = 0.791, Continuance = 0.792 and for Normative = 0.851. Overall alpha value for combined data was 0.823. The data was normally distributed since skewness for all the three constructs was: 0.3, 0.4 and 0.4 respectively. Mean, mode and median all were almost same for all the three constructs (Descriptive Statistics) parametric tests were applicable (t, ANOVA). Outliers were checked with the help of box plot and line charts. A structure model fit was done with the help of AMOS. Factor loading and the model fit values indicates the validity of the model developed. Sample size was 99.

4 Data Analysis and Interpretation

Table 1. Demographic data of the respondents

		Data	Percentage
Age	0–5 years	15	15
	5–10 years	12	12
	10–15years	27	27
	15 years and above	45	46
Gender	Male	75	76
	Female	24	24
Marital Status	Married	93	94
	Unmarried	06	06
Educational Qualification	Post Graduate	33	33
	Doctorate	66	67
Designation	Professor	15	15
	Associate Professor	27	27
	Assistant Professor	54	55
	Protem Lecturar	3	3

The demographic description of the respondents is mentioned as above (Table 1).

H_{01}: The relationship between the marital status and (the construct) Affective is significant
H_{02}: The relationship between the marital status and (the construct) Continuance is significant

H_{03}: The relationship between the marital status and (the construct) Normative is significant (Table 2)

Table 2. Analyzing the effect between constructs and the marital status (Two tailed unequal variance t- test

S. No.	Factors	Marital Status	Mean	Stand Dev.	N	d.f.	t	P. Value	t-Criti.
1.	Affective	Married	3.95	0.4	93	6	- 0.76	0.48	2.45
		Unmarried	4.06	0.35	6				
2	Continuance	Married	3.84	0.422	93	6	0.13	0.90	2.45
		Unmarried	3.81	0.48	6				
3	Normative	Married	3.84	0.46	93	14	- 3.92	0.00	2.14
		Unmarried	4.13	0.14	6				

Groups	Count	Sum	Average	Variance
0-5 years	15	55.875	3.725	0.156696
5-10 years	12	46.875	3.90625	0.011719
10-15 years	27	102.375	3.791667	0.147837
15 years and above	45	174.75	3.883333	0.248153

Interpretation-2: From the table above, t-critical > t-value, (2.45>-0.76) and p- at 5% level of significance is > 0.05 hence indicating that the marital status has an significant impact due to the first construct (affective). Similarly, p-value for continuance and Normative is > 0.05 hence null hypotheses for both is accepted.

H_{04}: The relationship between the Genders and (the construct) Affective is significant
H_{05}: The relationship between the Genders and (the construct) Continuance is significant
H_{06}: The relationship between the Genders and (the construct) Normative is significant
(Table 3)

Table 3. Effect between constructs and the genders (Two tailed unequal variance t- test)

S. No.	Factors	Gender	Mean	Stand Devi.	N	d.f.	t	P-value	t-Crit.
1	Affective	Male	4	0.41	75	46	1.79	0.08	2.01
		Female	3.84	0.35	24				
2	Continuance	Male	3.85	0.44	75	46	0.59	0.56	2.01
		Female	3.80	0.36	24				
3	Normative	Male	3.84	0.45	75	38	−0.82	0.41	2.02
		Female	3.92	0.45	24				

Interpretation-3: It is evident that p-value exceed 0.005, and t-critical > t-values calculated in all the three cases, hence states that the stated hypothesis is accepted in all the three conditions.

H_{07}: The relationship between the different level of experience and the Affective constructs is significant.
H_{08}: The relationship between the different level of experience and the Continuance construct is significant
H_{09}: The relationship between the different level of experience and the Normative construct is significant (Table 4)

Table 4. Different level of experience and affective commitment-ANOVA single factor

Groups	Count	Sum	Average	Variance
0-5 years	15	58.125	3.875	0.073661
5-10 years	12	47.25	3.9375	0.046875
10-15 years	27	110.625	4.097222	0.10016
15 years and above	45	175.875	3.908333	0.241761

Source of Variation	SS	df	MS	F	P-value	F crit
Between Groups	0.742708	3	0.247569	1.590359	0.19683	2.70041
Within Groups	14.78854	95	0.155669			
Total	15.53125	98				

Interpretation 4: P-value exceeding 0.05 and F critical is more than F calculated, hence indicates that the relationship between the different age groups and the Continuance construct is significant. It can be said that the employees of different level of experience have different level of continuance commitment (Table 5).

Table 5. Different level of experience and continuance commitment-ANOVA single factor

Source of Variation	SS	df	MS	F	P-value	F crit
B/W Groups	0.742708	3	0.247569	1.590359	0.19683	2.70041
Within Groups	14.78854	95	0.155669			
Total	15.53125	98				

Source of Variation	SS	df	MS	F	P-value	F crit
B/W Groups	0.397798	3	0.132599	0.737304	0.532345	2.700409
Within Groups	17.08516	95	0.179844			
Total	17.48295	98				

Interpretation 5: P-value (0.532) > 0.05, and F critical > F calculated, hence the null hypothesis is not disapproved, indicating that that the respondents of different experience have different level of continuance commitment towards the organizations. It changes with experience. The continuity of the employees depends on many factors (Table 6).

Table 6. Different level of experience and normative commitment-ANOVA single factor

Groups	Count	Sum	Average	Variance
0-5 years	15	58.5	3.9	0.089732
5-10 years	12	47.25	3.9375	0.004261
10-15 years	27	102.75	3.805556	0.23117
15 years and above	45	173.25	3.85	0.271023

Source of Variation	SS	df	MS	F	P-value	F crit
B/w Groups	0.179072	3	0.059691	0.294753	0.8291	2.700409
Within Groups	19.23854	95	0.202511			
Total	19.41761	98				

Interpretation 6: P-value (0.8291) > 0.05 and F $_{critical}$ > F $_{calculated}$. It indicates that the normative commitment is different of employees having different level of experience. We accept the null hypothesis, it also suggests that as the experience increases the different commitment of the employee's changes or differs.

H_{10}: The relationship between the educational level and the Affective construct is significant

H_{11}: The relationship between the educational level and the Continuance construct is significant

H_{12}: The relationship between the educational level and the Normative construct is significant (Table 7).

Table 7. Education and affective commitment -ANOVA single factor

Groups	Count	Sum	Average	Variance
Doctrate	66	259.125	3.926136	0.148066
Post-Graduate	33	132.75	4.022727	0.178178

Source of Variation	SS	df	MS	F	P-value	F crit
B/w Groups	0.205255682	1	0.20525	1.29908	0.25718	3.93912
Within Groups	15.32599432	97	0.158			
Total	15.53125	98				

Interpretation 7: The data indicates that since the P-value (0.2571 > 0.05 and $F_{critical}$ > $F_{calculated}$ again hence educational level and the Affective construct's relationships is significant. Shows that different educational levels of the respondents have different levels of affective commitments towards the organizations, Average and variance values indicates that the Post-Graduates commitments varies more than the Doctorates (Table 8).

Table 8. Education and Continuance commitment -ANOVA single factor

Groups	Count	Sum	Average	Variance
Doctrate	66	252.75	3.829545	0.175306
Post-Graduate	33	127.125	3.852273	0.189897

Source of Variation	SS	df	MS	F	P-value	F crit
B/w Groups	0.011363636	1	0.011364	0.063089	0.802209	3.939126
Within Groups	17.47159091	97	0.180119			
Total	17.48295455	98				

Interpretation 8: On the basis of above analyzed data, the relationship between the educational level and the Continuance construct is not similar. Average in this case is similar for both doctorates and Post-Graduates but the variance of PG- respondents is bit more (Table 9).

Table 9. Education and normative commitment-ANOVA single factor

Groups	Count	Sum	Average	Variance
Doctorate	66	253.125	3.835227	0.186615
Post-Graduate	33	128.625	3.897727	0.225053

Source of Variation	SS	df	MS	F	P-value	F crit
Between Groups	0.0859375	1	0.085938	0.431206	0.512953	3.939126
Within Groups	19.33167614	97	0.199296			
Total	19.41761364	98				

Interpretation 9: The relationship between the educational level and the normative construct is significant i.e. the people of different educational backgrounds have different levels of normative commitment levels towards an organization.

Table 10 indicates the factor loading. The above table indicates the 24 questions of the three constructs (8 each) and their estimates. (Tool used AMOS)

Table 10. Standardized regression weights: (Group number 1 - Default model (A = Affective commitment, CON = Continuance commitment and NOR = Normative Commitment)

			Estimates
A1	<---	A	.506
A2	<---	A	.167
A3	<---	A	.456
A4	<---	A	.294
A5	<---	A	.910
A6	<---	A	.941
A7	<---	A	.590
A8	<---	A	.622
CON1	<---	Con	.778
CON2	<---	Con	.577
CON3	<---	Con	.696
CON4	<---	Con	.714
CON5	<---	Con	.419
CON6	<---	Con	.506
CON7	<---	Con	.753
CON8	<---	Con	.505
NOR8	<---	Nor	.583
NOR7	<---	Nor	.551
NOR6	<---	Nor	.915
NOR5	<---	Nor	.781
NOR4	<---	Nor	.634
NOR3	<---	Nor	.565
NOR2	<---	Nor	.680
NOR1	<---	Nor	.697

Table 11. Model fit values

CMIN/ d.f.	NFI	TLI	CFI	RMSEA	PCLOSE
5.835	0.386	0.361	0.424	0.222	0

The value of CMIN/d.f. is 5.835, is acceptable. The values in the above table indicate the goodness of fit of the data (Table 11).

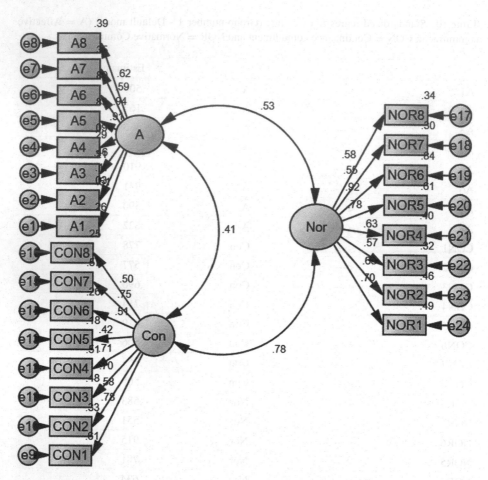

Conclusion: The success of the organization entirely depends upon the committed workforce. It leads to achieving the organizational objectives and goals, it helps to undertake risk and take sound decision. This helps the organization to sustain people in the organization. To assess the impact of demographic profile like age, gender, marital status, educational qualification and designation on the OC of the faculty. The relationship between the constructs and the marital status i.e. Affective, Continuance and Normative is significant. Same was the case with the genders; experience and education with the factors are significant. It hence indicates that all the three constructs have equal impact or the same relationship with the different constructs. The finding of the study can be applicable in every sector and can help in enhancing the commitment level of the employees. It becomes important for the organization management to understand the different demographic factors associated with the employees. The study also revealed that the administration of the educational institutes must focus on the HR practices to improve and enhance the commitment levels of the employees in the Higher education institutes of Uttarakhand. It was also revealed in the study that the employee's demographic characteristics are a very important determining factor of the commitment of the employees.

References

Mathieu, J.E., Zajac, D.M.: A review and meta-analysis of the antecedents, correlates, and consequences of organizational commitment. Psychol. Bull. **108**(2), 171–194 (1990). https://doi.org/10.1037/0033-2909.108.2.171

Meyer, J.P., Allen, N.J.: Commitment in the Workplace: Theory, Research, and Application. Sage Publications, Inc. (1997)

Porter, L.W., Steers, R.M., Mowday, R.T., Boulian, P.V.: Organizational commitment, job satisfaction, and turnover among psychiatric technicians. J. Appl. Psychol. **59**(5), 603–609 (1974). https://doi.org/10.1037/h0037335

Buchanan, B.: Building organizational commitment: the socialization of managers in work organizations. Adm. Sci. Q. **19**, 533–546 (1974). https://doi.org/10.2307/2391809

Shah, I.A., Fakhr, Z., Ahmad, M.S., Zaman, K.: Measuring push, pull and personal factors affecting turnover intention: a case of university teachers in Pakistan. Rev. Econ. Bus. Study **3**(1), 167–192 (2010)

Bhatnagar, J.: Predictors of organizational commitment in India: strategic HR roles, organizational learning capability and psychological empowerment. Int. J. Hum. Resour. Manag. **18**(10), 1782–1811 (2007)

Suki, N.M., Suki, N.M.: Job satisfaction and organizational commitment: the effect of gender. Int. J. Psychol. Res. **6**(5), 1-p15 (2011)

Iqbal, A., Kokash, H.A., Al-Oun, S.: The impact assessment of demographic factors on faculty commitment in the kingdom of Saudi Arabian universities. J. Coll. Teach. Learn. **8**(2), 1–14 (2011)

Yucel, I., Bektas, C.: Job satisfaction, organizational commitment and demographic characteristics among teachers in Turkey: younger is better? Procedia – Soc. Behav. Sci. **46**, 1598–1608 (2012)

Elkhdr, H., Kanbur, A.: Organizational commitment in relation to demographic characteristics among lecturers working at Libyan universities. Int. J. Hum. Soc. Sci. Invention **7**(12), 46–52 (2018)

Viet, V.V.: Demographic factors affecting organizational commitment of lecturers. VNU J. Sci. Educ. Res. **31**(4), 16–25 (2015)

Bashir, B., Gani, A.: Correlates of organisational commitment among university teachers in India: an empirical investigation. Asia-Pacific J. Manag. Res. Innov. **16**(1), 7–20 (2020)

Tandon, P., Mishra, S., Mehta, J.D.: A study on demographic variables and organizational commitment of employees. Int. J. Manag. **11**(9), 1416–1424 (2020)

Agrawal, S., Jain, B.K.: Influence of demographic variables on organizational commitment of school teachers: evidence from the Kathmandu Valley Nepa. Quest J. Manag. Soc. Sci. **2**(2), 262–274 (2020)

Govindaraju, N.: Demographic factors influence on employee retention. Int. J. Eng. Stud. Tech. Approach **4**(7), 11–20 (2018)

Sandhu, D., Kapoor, A.: Impact of Demographic Variables on Organizational Commitment: A Study amongst College Teachers. Int. J. Sci. Res. **6**(5), 295–296 (2017)

Yadav, S., Srivasatava, N.: A study on the relationship between demographic variables and employee engagement. Psychol. Educ. **58**(2), 7950–7954 (2021)

Gopinath, R.: The influence of demographic factors on the job involvement, organisational commitment and job satisfaction of academic leaders in the Tamil Nadu universities. Eur. J. Mol. Clin. Med. **7**(3), 5056–5067 (2020)

Prostate Cancer Data Analytics Using Hybrid ECNN and ERNN Techniques

Asadi Srinivasulu[1]([⊠]), Anand Kumar Gupta[2], Swapnil B. Kolambakar[3],
Madhusudana Subramanyam[4], Siva Ram Rajeyyagari[5], Tarkeshwar Barua[6],
and Asadi Pushpa[7]

[1] BlueCrest University, 1000 Monrovia, Liberia
head.research@bluecrest.edu.lr
[2] Data Science Research Lab, BlueCrest University, 1000 Monrovia, Liberia
anand.gupta@bluecrestcollege.com
[3] OpenLabs, BlueCrest University, 1000 Monrovia, Liberia
[4] Department of CS and Engineering, KL University, Guntur, Andhra Pradesh, India
mmsnaidu@kluniversity.in
[5] Department of CS and IT, Shaqra University, Shaqra, Saudi Arabia
dr.sivaram@su.edu.sa
[6] REGex Software Services, Jaipur, India
tarkeshwar.b@regexsoftware.com
[7] ECE Department, S.V University, Tirupati, A.P., India

Abstract. Prostate is a subsequent driving reasons for malignant growth passings among male human. Primal location of malignant tumor can actually lessen the pace of deathrate brought about by Prostatic malignant growth. Because of high and multi-resolution of MRIs from prostatic malignant growth require a legitimate demonstrative frameworks and instruments. In the foregone specialists created Computer supported finding (CAD) frameworks that assist the radiologist with distinguishing the irregularities. In this exploration paper, we have utilized novel Deep Learning methods like Hybrid ECNN-ERNN. Convolutional Neural Networks and Recurrent Neural Networks for distinguishing prostate cancer. In addition, various elements extricating techniques are proposed to further develop the location execution. The highlights removing methodologies depend on surface, morphological, scale invariant element change (SIFT), and elliptic Fourier descriptors (EFDs) highlights. The exhibition was assessed in light of single as well as mix of elements utilizing Deep Learning Classification strategies. The Cross approval (Jack-blade k-crease) was performed and execution was assessed in term of get working bend (ROC) and particularity, responsiveness, Positive prescient worth (PPV), negative prescient worth (NPV), misleading positive rate (FPR). In view of single highlights separating methodologies, ECNN procedure gives the most elevated precision of 98.34% with AUC of 0.999. While, utilizing mix of highlights removing procedures, ECNN with surface + morphological, and EFDs + morphological elements give the most noteworthy precision of 99.71% and AUC of 1.00. The proposed model outperformed than the existing system with parameters / metrics as accuracy (82.42%), error rate (0.13), val_loss (0.41), val_accuracy (0.50), size of dataset used in research (1.50 GB), No. of epochs (30), Time-complexity ($O(n^2)$) and execution time (1022 ms).

Keywords: Prostate cancer · Autoencoders · Deep learning · Cancer prediction · CNN · RNN · ECNN · ERNN · Data minelaying · Feature selection · Data pre-processing

1 Introduction

Prostate malignant growth (PCa) is the third most usually analyzed cancer around the world, after lung and bosom cancer and the fifth reason for malignant growth explicit passing in guys [1]. Around 191,930 patients will be determined to have PCa in 2020 in the United States, with an expected 33,330 passings [2]. Over the most recent couple of years, research was centered around finding, guess and forecast of PCa results taking a jump using Statistics and Artificial Intelligence (AI). The utilization of PC based learning models has turned into a transcendent area of exploration in PCa. Counterfeit Neural Networks (ANN) have progressively been utilized to fabricate progressed prognostic models for PCa [3]. To prepare an AI model it is sufficient to procure organized datasets including input factors and results, with little information on the PCa experiences. For example, a few novel instruments are accessible for screening and conclusion of PCa, for example, genomics, attractive reverberation imaging (MRI) and biomarkers (exosomes and sub-atomic imaging). In this situation, AI might play an essential part, first in the translation of this colossal measure of information, second in the improvement of AI calculations that might be useful to urologists to diminish the quantity of superfluous prostate biopsies without missing the finding of forceful PCa. Besides, the utilization of genomics, AI and extracellular vesicles [4] (exosomes and without cell DNA from body liquids), can give a more dependable and faster PCa test [4, 5].

2 Literature Survey

The software engineering plans to fabricate brilliant gadgets performing undertakings that at present require human knowledge. Through AI (ML), the profound learnedness (DL) model is training PCs to advance as a visual demonstration, something that people are doing normally. Simulated intelligence is reforming medical services. Computerized pathology is turning out to be exceptionally helped by AI to help specialists in breaking down bigger informational indexes and giving quicker and more precise analyses of prostate cancer sores. When practical to analytic imagination, AI has shown amazing precision in the location of prostatic sores as well as in the expectation of forbearing results concerning endurance and treatment reaction. The tremendous amount of information coming from the prostate cancer genome requires quick, solid and precise registering power given by AI calculations. Radiotherapy is a fundamental piece of the therapy of prostate cancer and anticipating its harmfulness for the patients is frequently troublesome. Man-made brainpower could play a future potential part in foreseeing how a patient will respond to the treatment secondary effects. These advancements could furnish specialists with amended bits of knowledge on the most proficient method to design radiation therapy treatment. The augmentation of the abilities of careful mechanism for additional independent assignments will permit them to utilize data from the careful field, perceive issues and execute the appropriate activities without the requirement for humanlike intercession [2].

3   Research Methodology

3.1   Existing System

There are two distinct techniques are available and used by scholars of deep learning as CNN and RNN [1, 3]. These methods are indeed vast used, and produce great outcomes though these techniques have following drawbacks (Table 1):

Table 1. Disadvantages of CNN and RNN techniques

CNN:	RNN:
▪ Less accuracy, and less precision ▪ High error rate ▪ High time complexity ▪ Unable to handle Big data	▪ Inefficient to detect small-data objects ▪ Good to predict data label, not suitable for segmentation ▪ Less precision, and less accuracy ▪ High error prone

3.2   Proposed System

This research work focuses to avoid the existing drawbacks of CNN-RNN techniques. This enhanced prototype combines CNN-RNN technique in such a way to produce a hybrid model to achieve the following advantages (Table 2):

Table 2. Advantages of proposed ECNN and ERNN techniques

ECNN:	ERNN:
▪ High accuracy, and high precision ▪ Less error rates ▪ Less time complexity ▪ Handles Big data	▪ Detects small-data object easily ▪ Great for data segmentation and prediction ▪ High precision, and accuracy ▪ Less error prone

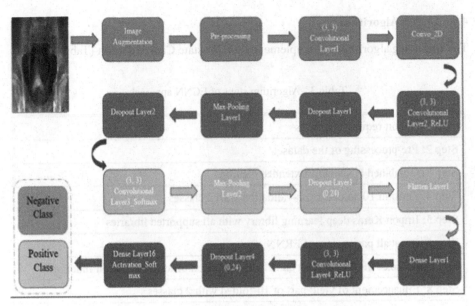

Fig. 1. Proposed architecture of ECNN technique

The above Fig. 1 describes the proposed architecture for Prostate Cancer prediction and detection using ECNN.

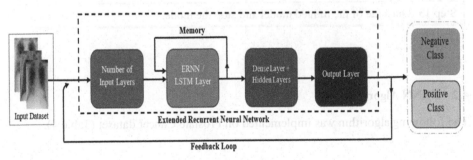

Fig. 2. Proposed architecture of ERNN technique

The above Fig. 2 explains the proposed architecture for Prostate Cancer prediction and detection using ERNN.

4   Experimental Results

The implemented combined techniques of ECNN-ERNN were applied on Prostate Cancer dataset of 16,733 x-ray images (1.75 GB) and produced significant results with an accuracy of 92%.

4.1 ECNN Algorithm

The following algorithm was implemented on Prostate Cancer dataset (Table 3).

Table 3. Algorithm steps of ECNN approach

Step 1: Import required libraries
Step 2: Pre-processing of the dataset
Step 3: Combined RNN with Extended Neurons
Step 4: Perform 10-folded cross-validation with 2 classes
Step 5: Import Keras deep learning library with all supported libraries
Step 6: Reset all parameters of ERNN
Step 7: Enhance the ECNN part and about regulation of loss calculation function
Step 8: Enhancement of yield part of 10-folded with 2 classes
Step 9: Accumulate the ERNN parameters
Step 10: Adjusting the ERNN in the preparation of model
Step 11: Load the Omicron disease infection image dataset
Step 12: Predicting the infection severity through classifying the dataset into 2 classes
Step 13: Outcome of the trained model and stop the model

4.2 ERNN Algorithm

The following algorithm was implemented on Prostate Cancer dataset (Table 4).

Table 4. Algorithm steps of ERNN approach

Step 1: Import required library
Step 2: Pre-processing of the dataset
Step 3: Combined CNN with Extended Neurons
Step 4: Perform 10 folded cross validation with 2 classes
Step 5: Import Keras deep learning library with all supported libraries
Step 6: Reset all parameters of ECNN
Step 7: Enhance the ECNN part and about regulation of loss calculation function
Step 8: Enhancement of yield part of 10 folded with 2 classes
Step 9: Accumulate the ECNN parameters
Step 10: Adjusting the ECNN in the preparation of model
Step 11: Load the Monkeypox disease infection image dataset
Step 12: Predicting the infection severity through classifying the dataset into 2 classes
Step 13: Outcome of the trained model and stop the model

The following formulas were used to calculate the accuracy of the proposed model (Fig. 3).

$$S_{ij} = (I * K)_{ij} = \sum_{a=\lfloor -\frac{m}{2} \rfloor}^{\lfloor \frac{m}{2} \rfloor} \sum_{b=\lfloor -\frac{n}{2} \rfloor}^{\lfloor \frac{n}{2} \rfloor} I_{i-a,j-b} K_{\frac{m}{2}+a,\frac{n}{2}+b} \rightarrow (1)$$

Fig. 3. Equation used in proposed architecture

4.3 Input Datset

The below furnished is the input image dataset used in this proposed research work (Fig. 4).

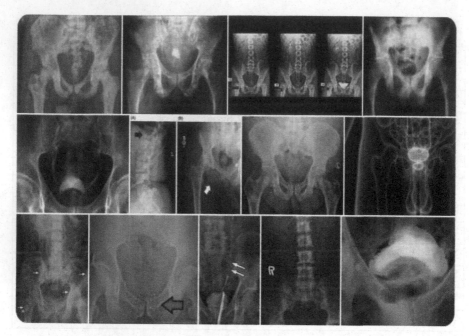

Fig. 4. Input dataset

5   Results

Here is the result of in finding Prostate cancer detection by integrating ECNN.

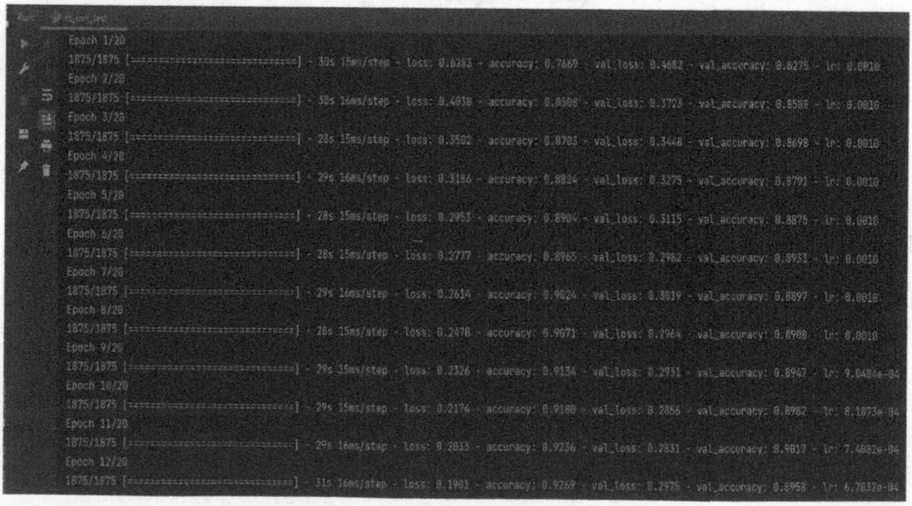

Fig. 5. Executing flow of ECNN

Figure 5 Exemplify the executing rate of flow through with Epochs on Prostate Malignant tumor dataset

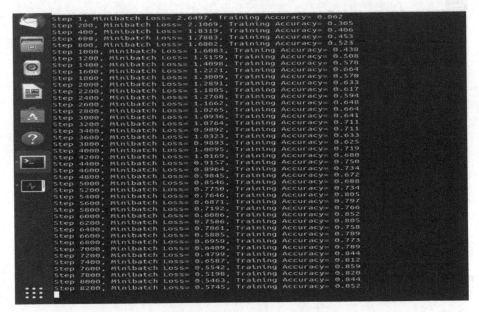

Fig. 6. Executing flow of ERNN

Figure 6 Exemplify the execution flow through Epochs on Prostate Cancer dataset

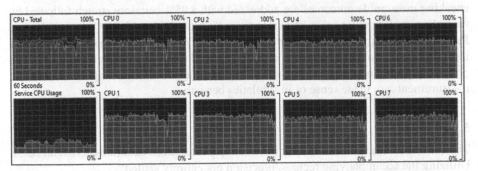

Fig. 7. CPU occupancy in the executing of ECNN with Windows OS

In the above Fig. 7 it demonstrates the Processor occupancy rendering to the iterations with Epoches onto Prostate Cancer virus dataset with Windows OS.

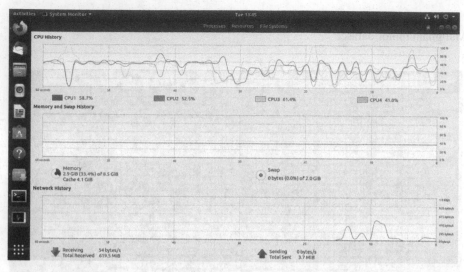

Fig. 8. CPU occupancy for prostate cancer dataset using ERNN

In the above Fig. 8 it exemplifies processing power occupancy rendering to the number of Epochs on Prostate Cancer illness with Linux OS.

5.1 Performance Evaluation Methods

The in general trial result is estimated and introduced utilizing the most broadly utilized factual methodologies, for example, exactness, accuracy, review, F1-score, responsiveness, and particularity. For Study One, because of the restricted examples, the generally speaking measurable outcomes are addressed with a 95% certainty stretch followed by recently revealed writing that likewise utilized a little dataset [20, 24]. In our dataset, Prostate Cancer may be delegated genuine positive (Tp) or genuine negative (Tn) assuming people are analyzed precisely, and it very well may be characterized into bogus positive (Fp) or misleading pessimistic (Fn) if misdiagnosed. The assigned measurable measurements are made sense of in subtleties beneath.

5.1.1 Accuracy

The exactness is the general number of effectively recognized occasions across all cases. Utilizing the accompanying recipes, precision not entirely settled:

$$Accuracy = \frac{T_p + T_n}{T_p + T_n + F_p + F_n}$$

5.1.2 Preciseness

Precision is evaluated as the proportion of precisely anticipated positive results out of completely anticipated positive results.

$$Precision = \frac{T_p}{T_p + F_p}$$

5.1.3 Recall

Recall alludes to the proportion of significant results that the calculation precisely distinguishes.

$$Recall = \frac{T_p}{T_n + F_p}$$

5.1.4 Sensitivity

Sensitivity alludes to the main exact positive metric comparative with the complete number of events and can be estimated as follows:

$$Sensitivity = \frac{T_p}{T_p + F_n}$$

5.1.5 Specificity

It distinguishes the quantity of precisely recognized and determined genuine negatives and can be tracked down utilizing the accompanying recipe:

$$Specificity = \frac{T_n}{T_n + F_p}$$

5.1.6 F1- Score

F1-evaluation: The F1 rating is the symphonious mean of accuracy and review. The greatest conceivable F score is 1, which shows amazing review and accuracy.

$$F1 - Score = 2 \times \frac{Precision \times Recall}{Precision + Recall}$$

5.1.7 Area Under Curve (AUC)

The region under the bend (AUC) addresses the way of behaving of the models under different circumstances. AUC can be determined suing following equations:

$$AUC = \Sigma ri(Xp) - Xp$$

5.2 Evaluation Metrics

Metrics are used to find and evaluate accuracy, precision, time complexity and execution time etc.

$$Quality = \frac{BP + VM}{BP + VP + BM + VM}$$

$$Preciseness = \frac{BP}{BP + VP}$$

$$Callback = \frac{BP}{BP + VM}$$

$$F - measure = \frac{2 \times Preciseness \times Callback}{Preciseness + Callback}$$

5.3 Data Input

As previously said, our experiment will consider 6098 images.

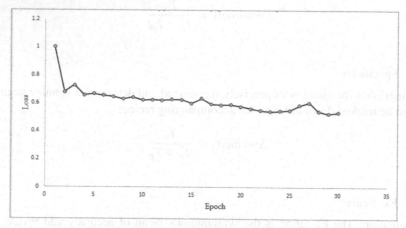

Fig. 9. Prostate cancer ECNN data epochs vs. loss

Figure 9 Exemplify the executing epochs between Epochs and Loss.

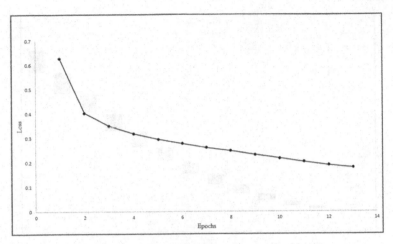

Fig. 10. Prostate cancer ERNN data epochs vs. loss

Figure 10 Exemplify the executing epochs between Epochs and Loss.

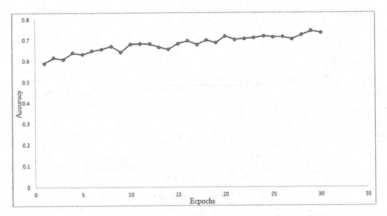

Fig. 11. Prostate cancer ERNN data epochs vs. loss

Figure 11 Exemplify the executing epochs between Epochs and Loss.

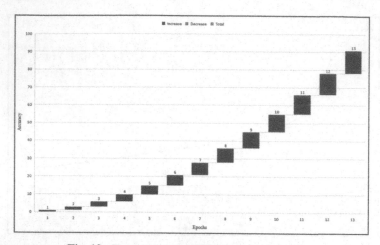

Fig. 12. Prostate cancer ERNN data epochs vs. loss

Figure 12 Exemplify the executing epochs between Epochs and Loss.

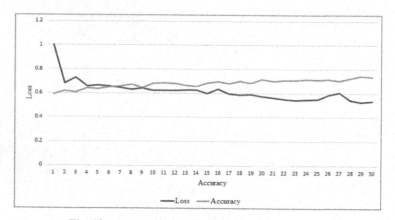

Fig. 13. Prostate cancer ECNN data accuracy vs. loss

Figure 13 Exemplify the executing epochs between Accuracy and Loss.

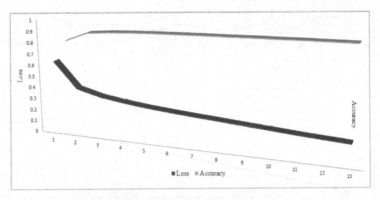

Fig. 14. Prostate cancer ECNN data accuracy vs. loss

Figure 14 Exemplify the executing epochs between Accuracy and Loss (Fig. 15).

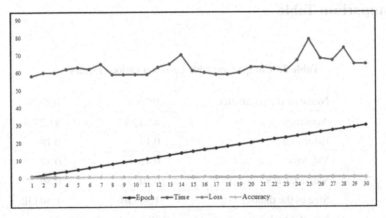

Fig. 15. Prostate cancer ERNN data epochs vs. loss

Figure 16 Exemplify the executing epochs between Epochs and Loss.

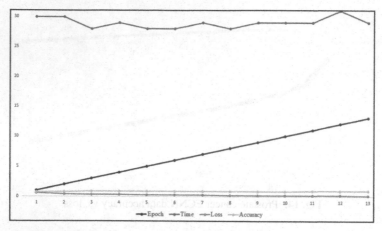

Fig. 16. Prostate cancer ERNN data epochs vs. loss

6 Comparison Table

Table 5. Comparison table based on various factors

Sl. No.	Name of the parameter	ECNN	ERNN
1.	Accuracy	82.42%	91.27%
2.	Error rate	0.13	0.18
3.	Val_loss	0.41	0.37
4.	Val_accuracy	0.50	0.80
5.	Size of the dataset	1.50 GB	1.50 GB
6.	No. of epochs	30	30
7.	Time-complexity	$O(n^2)$	$O(n^2)$
8.	Execution time	1022 ms	1250 ms

The Table 5 explains the comparison factors of the both techniques based on multiple parameters.

7 Conclusions

In this experimentation, the vigorous DL (Deep learning) grouping procedures, for example, ECNN calculation, ERNN approach and ELSTM are utilized to order the malignant tumor from the Brachytherapy. High goals pictures show high non-linear elements that is require a complex element extricating procedures to recognize cancer from picture because of enormous variety in size shape require multiple layer highlights separating techniques to separate the malignant growth successfully. Consequently, to deal with this issue, various highlights extricating procedures are utilized, for example, scale invariant component change (SIFT), surface, biological science and elliptic Fourier descriptors (EFDs). To recognize the Brachytherapy from the Prostate malignant growth, the original DL characterization methods, for example, ECNN and its calculation, ELSTM and Bayes approaching are created in Matlab rendition 2017. The Transverse approval (Jack-knife 10-crease) was utilized to prepare and test the MR picture information base. The exhibition was assessed utilizing a few measures (particularity, responsiveness, PPV, NPV, FPR and AUC). Both single and blend of highlights removing techniques are formulated to assess the exhibition. The higher arrangement precision in view of single surface and morphological highlights were acquired utilizing ECNN calculation, though, mix of various elements, for example, morphologic with EFDs and surface supply more exactness than single component precedes by surface component with selective information and EFDs utilizing ECNN calculation, DTs, and Bayes approaching. Before, the specialists utilize just scarcely any single highlights-based technique and barely any joined elements to recognize the prostate malignant growth. In any case, the outcome announced in this study uncovered that the ongoing elements removing technique is more powerful to analyze and distinguish the prostate malignant growth in recognizing the explicitness and awareness for gaining higher identification proportion of prostate cancer

A portion of the limitations associated with our work can be overwhelmed by refreshing the dataset by ceaselessly gathering new Prostate Cancer tainted patient pictures, assessing the proposed ECNN-ERNN model's exhibition on exceptionally imbalanced information, contrasting the presentation of our model and other specialists' discoveries (once accessible), and send our proposed model in creating versatile based conclusion device. The proposed model i.e., ERNN outperformed than the existing system with parameters / metrics as accuracy (91.27%), error rate (0.18), val_loss (0.37), val_accuracy (0.80), size of dataset used in research (1.50 GB), No. of epochs (30), Time-complexity ($O(n^2)$) and execution time (1250 ms).

References

1. Abbasi, A.A., et al.: Detecting prostate cancer using deep learning convolution neural network with transfer learning approach. Cogn. Neurodyn. **14**(4), 523–533 (2020). https://doi.org/10.1007/s11571-020-09587-5
2. Hussain, L., et al.: Prostate cancer detection using machine learning techniques by employing combination of features extracting strategies, 393–413 (2018)
3. Tataru, O.S., et al.: Artificial intelligence and machine learning in prostate cancer patient management—current trends and future perspectives. Diagnostics **11**, 354 (2021). https://doi.org/10.3390/diagnostics11020354
4. Bray, F., Ferlay, J., Soerjomataram, I., Siegel, R.L., Torre, L.A., Jemal, A.: Global cancer statistics 2018: GLOBOCAN estimates of incidence and mortality worldwide for 36 cancers in 185 countries. CA Cancer J. Clin. **68**, 394–424 (2018)
5. Siegel, R.L., et al.: Colorectal cancer statistics. CA Cancer J. Clin. **67**, 177–193 (2017). https://doi.org/10.3322/776caac.21395
6. Siegel, R.L., et al.: Cancer Statistics. CA Cancer J. Clin. **70**, 7–30 (2020)

7. Chou, R., et al.: Screening for prostate cancer: a review of the evidence for the U.S. preventive services task force. Ann. Intern. Med. **155**, 375–386 (2011)
8. Jović, S., Miljković, M., Ivanović, M., Šaranović, M., Arsić, M.: Prostate cancer probability prediction by machine learning technique. Cancer Investig. **35**, 647–651 (2017)
9. Bashir, M.N.: Epidemiology of prostate cancer. Asian Pacific J. Cancer Prev. **16**, 5137–5141 (2015). https://doi.org/10.7314/APJCP.2015.16.13.5137
10. Pang, B., et al.: Extracellular vesicles: the next generation of biomarkers for liquid biopsy-based prostate cancer diagnosis. Theranostics **10**, 2309–2326 (2020)
11. Ohori, M., Wheeler, T.M., Scardino, P.T.: The new American joint committee on cancer and international union against cancer TNM classification of prostate cancer. Cancer **73**, 104–794 (1994). https://doi.org/10.1002/1097-0142(19940701)74:1<104::AID-CNCR2820740119>3.0.CO;2-5
12. Yadav, K.K.: How AI Is Optimizing the Detection and Management of Prostate Cancer. IEEE Pulse **9**, 19 (2018)
13. Talcott, J.A., et al.: Using patient-reported outcomes to assess and improve prostate cancer brachytherapy. BJU Int. **114**, 511–516 (2014). https://doi.org/10.1111/bju.12464
14. Russell, S.J., Norvig, P.: Artificial Intelligence: A Modern Approach. Prentice Hall, Upper Saddle River, NJ, USA (2009). ISBN 0-13-207148-7
15. Kattan, M.W., et al.: CME article brachytherapy in prostate cancer. Urology **4295**, 393–399 (2001)
16. Goldenberg, S.L., Nir, G., Salcudean, S.E.: A new era: artificial intelligence and machine learning in prostate cancer. Nat. Rev. Urol. **16**, 391–403 (2019)
17. Rathore, S., Hussain, M., Khan, A.: Automated colon cancer detection using hybrid of novel geometric features and some traditional features. Comput. Biol. Med. **65**, 279–296 (2015). https://doi.org/10.1016/j.compbiomed.2015.03.004
18. Goodfellow, I., Bengio, Y., Courville, A., Bengio, Y.: Deep Learning, vol. 1. MIT Press, Cambridge, UK (2016)
19. Yu, K.K., Hricak, H.: Imaging prostate cancer. J. Urol. **38**(809), 59–85 (2000). https://doi.org/10.1016/S0033-8389(05)70150-0
20. Hussain, L., et al.: Prostate cancer detection using machine learning techniques by employing combination of features extracting strategies. Cancer Biomark. **21**, 393–413 (2018)
21. Schröder, F.H., et al.: Screening and prostate-cancer mortality in a randomized European study. N. Engl. J. Med. **360**, 1320–1328 (2009). https://doi.org/10.1056/NEJMoa0810084

A Review on Smart Patient Monitoring and Management in Orthopaedics Using Machine Learning

Puneet Kaur[1], Kiranbir Kaur[1], Kuldeep Singh[2], Prabhsimran Singh[1(✉)], and Salil Bharany[1]

[1] Department of Computer Engineering & Technology, Guru Nanak Dev University, Amritsar, India
{puneetcet.rsh,prabhsimran.dcet}@gndu.ac.in, kiran.dcse@gndu.ac, prabh_singh32@yahoo.com

[2] Department of Electronics Technology, Guru Nanak Dev University, Amritsar, India
kuldeep.ece@gndu.ac.in

Abstract. Tremendous advances have occurred in the sphere of Artificial intelligence in the past years, particularly in the application of Machine learning. Machine learning and Artificial intelligence are both playing a crucial role in Healthcare Domain presently. The infusion of various Machine learning techniques and models in healthcare and patient monitoring has significantly increased and has become what is commonly referred to as Smart Healthcare. Orthopaedics is a branch of health in which Machine learning has gained more popularity and usage rigorously nowadays. Various Machine learning technologies are popularly being utilised in the field of bone and skeletal research. A review of the various Machine learning technologies and approaches being implemented and studied in this field of Orthopaedics and the use of several machine learning techniques for predicting and detecting bone fracture, detecting several bone related diseases as well as their usefulness in bone surgery is presented in this paper.

Keywords: Artificial intelligence · Machine learning · Orthopaedics · Prediction models · Smart patient monitoring

1 Introduction

Orthopaedics, often known as orthopaedic surgery, is a branch of medicine that deals with maintaining and regaining the skeletal system's functionality as well as the accompanying muscles, joints, and other bones. Modern orthopaedics now treats a variety of acquired and congenital skeletal abnormalities as well as the side effects of degenerative illnesses like osteoarthritis in addition to treating fractures, shattered bones, strained muscles, ligaments and tendons which get torn, and other traumatic injuries. Health issues can arise from disorders that impact the strength and flexibility of bones. The body has two different types of bones. The outer layer of the bones is made up of dense and compact cortical bones. The interior layer of the bones is made up of spongy,

R. Singh et al. (Eds.): ICBDA 2022, CCIS 1742, pp. 53–63, 2022.
https://doi.org/10.1007/978-3-031-23647-1_5

honeycomb-shaped trabecular or cancellous bones. A person's bone strength and flexibility may be impacted by an illness or condition. These diseases can develop for a number of reasons, such as genetics, environment, food, and infections. As a surgical specialty, orthopaedics involves a strong combination of clinical judgement, surgical prowess, and—most importantly—technical expertise. Power tools, 3-D printing, novel implants, additive manufacturing, etc. have all seen an emerging usage in orthopaedic treatment. The development of artificial intelligence (AI) and robotics is without a doubt the new disruptive force in orthopaedics in the present period [1].

Numerous medical domains, including bone research, mineral research etc. which include prognosis of osteoporosis, osteoarthritis, bone cancer, the detection/prediction of fractures using both clinical and imaging data, are rapidly implementing machine learning (ML) approaches. Numerous studies using ML techniques have been published in the field of bone and mineral research [2]. The foundation of AI development in healthcare is machine learning, and there are compelling arguments for optimism. Artificial intelligence and machine learning are steadily spreading throughout contemporary society, particularly in the healthcare sector. We all actively or inadvertently contribute to the growth of heaps of data i.e. big data by using various technologies such as smartphones, wearables, online shopping etc. The average doctor is now more "plugged-in" to the latest and modish technology environment with growing use of various technologies in the healthcare field. The nature of operating on crucial anatomical structures in surgery, in particular, inspires a need for improvements that might equalise effectiveness while operating, safety of patients, and outcomes of surgical procedures [3]. Machine learning has gained quite a popularity particularly in the orthopaedic field. The role of Machine learning and AI in this orthopaedic domain is discussed as follows:

(i)   Detection of Bone Fractures Using ML
(ii)   Fracture Prediction using ML
(iii) Bone Diseases and ML
(iv)   Bone Surgery and ML

2   Problems Related to Bones

Bone discomfort, lumps, and brittleness are examples of bone disorders. Cancer, circulatory issues, metabolic bone abnormalities, infections, overuse injuries, and cancer can all cause bone pain. Fractures and dislocations are common injuries that result in bone pain, and an underlying condition like osteoporosis, which causes the bones to shrink and weaken, can make these injuries worse. The density, or "bone mass," of our bones serves as a gauge for their health. A bone mineral density (BMD) test, for instance, can assist a doctor in determining the calcium content of bones and, consequently, the strength of our bones. Bone lumps can result from the incorrect healing of a bone fracture or they might develop on their own as a growth, like a tumour. A common indication of osteoporosis or malnutrition is brittle bones.

2.1 Bone Fracture

A break or discontinuity in a bone is known as a fracture (Fig. 1). High force impact or stress are majorly the causes for a substantial portion of bone fractures (Fig. 2). However, other medical diseases that weaken the bones, like osteoporosis and some forms of cancer, can also cause fractures. These are known as pathological fractures in medical terminology. A closed fracture is a break in the bone that does not cause nearby tissue injury or rip through the skin, as opposed to a compound fracture, which does both. Due to the possibility of infection, compound fractures are typically more dangerous than simple fractures. There are different types of fractures such as : Avulsion, Compression, Greenstick, Hairline, Intra-articular, Longitudinal, Oblique, Comminuted, Pathological, Stress, Transverse, Spiral fracture, Fracture dislocation and so on.

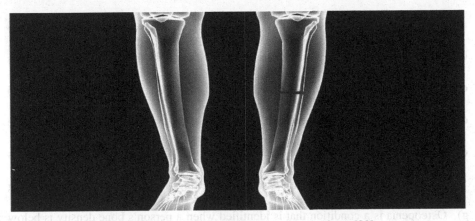

Fig. 1. Xray image of fractured vs healthy leg bone [28]

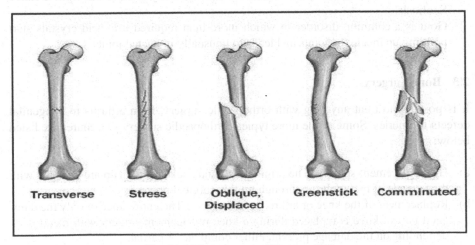

Fig. 2. Different types of Fracture [27]

2.2   Bone Diseases

Bone disorders can weaken bones, making them more brittle. Various types of bone issues include:

a) Osteoporosis and reduced bone density lead to brittle bones which can easily shatter.
b) Osteogenesis imperfecta makes bones weak and fragile.
c) Bones weakened by Paget's disease.
d) Bone Infections and cancer.
e) Some other bone issues can occur because of inadequate nutrition, genetically or rate of growth or reconstruction of bone.

Here are a few common bone diseases:

a) Osteoporosis is the most common bone disease which is characterised by density reduction, which makes the bones brittle, fragile, and readily breakable.
b) Osteomyelitis, another name for an infection of the bone tissue, is a rare but serious condition.
c) Osteoarthritis is a chronic degenerative joint condition, allowing the bones to rub against one another.
d) Bone tumours develop when cells inside the bones grow out of control and can be malignant too.
e) When Bone tissue dies in the absence of blood, that condition is called osteonecrosis and hence the bone becomes brittle and crumbles.
f) When the bone regeneration process (remodelling) happens too quickly, resulting in skeletal abnormalities then it is called Paget's disease.
g) Osteopenia is a condition that is identified when a person's bone density is below normal and hence also called Low bone density.
h) A disorder in which the spine's bones curve unnaturally to the left or right is called Scoliosis.
i) Gout is a common disorder in which more than required uric acid crystals start building up inside the joints and leads to unusually impacted joints.

2.3   Bone Surgery

It is possible to treat anything with orthopaedic surgery, from arthritis to congenital defects to injuries. Some of the more typical orthopaedic surgery procedures are listed below:

a) Hip replacement surgery: The original ball and socket of the Hip are changed with those made of metal/plastic throughout this surgical process.
b) Replacement of the knee or arthroscopic surgery: The entire knee or only the damaged part of knee is replaced during a knee replacement surgery with metal parts depending on the damage present, either complete or partial.

c) Surgery for the shoulder and rotator cuff: These procedures are very similar to those for the hip and knee in which shoulder's ball and socket, as well as just the injured portions, can be replaced with metal components (partial replacement).
d) Surgery on the wrist and hands: Because they are used so frequently in daily activities, the hands and wrists are susceptible to damage from accidents, ageing, and arthritis and orthopaedic surgeries can treat their damage too such as fracture and dislocation hands, wrists, fingers.
e) Anterior Cruciate Ligament, or ACL surgery: In this procedure, a tendon of another body part is utilised to make a duplicate and fresh ACL which is one of the knee's main ligaments.

3 Role of ML in Orthopaedics

This section is divided in four sub-sections and details of each is discussed below:

3.1 ML in Fracture Detection

In the field of Fracture detection using ML, Myint et al. [8] proposed an approach of machine learning for the detecting fracture of the leg bone by utilising X-ray images. In this process, unsharp masking was used to enhance the images and its edges. Then, Harris corner detection algorithm was used for corner features extraction from the processed images. The extracted features were fed to decision tree classifier for classification into fracture and non-fracture classes and kNN for classification into different fracture types such as normal, transverse, oblique and comminute. These classifiers provided accuracies of 92% and 83% for their respective tasks.

Similarly, Yadav et al. [9] proposed a feature fusion of CNN and canny edge algorithm to differentiate between a fractured and non fractured i.e. healthy bone. The composite scale fracture network(SF Net) worked with an improved canny edge algo and obtained edges to localise fracture region in images. The grey and the corresponding canny edge images were given as input to the SFNet for training and evaluating. The resulting outcome showed that SFNet + canny together achieve the highest accuracy of 99.12% for fracture detection.

In similar regards, Acici et al. [11] developed a framework for detection of femoral neck fractures using different ML approaches. CNN was used to extract LBP and HOG features from grey level images and LSTMS and BLLSTMS were fed. For optimisation, Metaheuristic algos, GA and PSO were used. The best performance for unbalanced dataset was provided by 2-layer LSTM architecture whereas for balanced was achieved by CNN architecture with PSO optimisation.

Also, Cao et al. [13] proposed a method which detects fracture for multiple bone fracture types. Stacked Random Forests Feature fusion was used for feature extraction from images produced by X-ray. The labels generated by class probability were used further to generate refined class distribution at another level. Fracture bounding boxes from most likely of containing a fracture to least likely of containing fracture was the result which were further evaluated on and the accuracy given out by the method was 81.2%.

Furthermore, Guan et al. [12] designed a new network by proposing a method, Dilated Convolutional feature pyramid network(DCFPN) for detecting fracture of the thigh bone. Dataset of 3842 thigh fracture radiographs was collected. The results depicted the Average precision of 82.1% of DCFPN in detecting thigh fractures.

As can be seen for, Hardalac et al. [10] conducted an experiment for detecting fracture of the wrist bone using X-ray images by the aid of ML. Various machine learning object detection models such as SABL, RegNet, RetinaNet, Libra R-CNN, Faster R-CNN, FSAF, Dynamic R-CNN, PAA and DCN were applied on dataset of wrist bone images and different group of models were used to develop a wrist fracture detection combo (WFD-C) model. An average precision (AP50) of 0.8639 was achieved by the WFD-C model.

3.2 ML in Fracture Prediction

In the prediction of fracture using ML technology, Kruse et al. [15] applied machine learning techniques for prediction of fractures of the hip bone and estimated Dual-energy X-ray absorptiometry (DXA). Data of patients including both male and female was combined with DXA absorptiometry data. In order to find out the area of the curve (AUC) and probability estimates, various models of statistics by using k-5, 5-repeat cross-validation were created on 2/3rd of the data points and then validated on the remaining 1/3rd. Based on test AUC 0.92 and probabilities which were accurately measured after modifications by Naive Bayes, Bootstrap aggregated flexible discriminant analysis (bagFDA) fared most relevant for women. The "bagFDA" model, which only considered 11 variables, produced an outcome AUC of 0.91. For men, a test AUC 0.89, eXtreme Gradient Boosting ("xgbTree") outperformed all, albeit with very bad calibration at greater probabilities. Using a subset of predictor, a "xgbTree" model produced a test AUC of 0.86 [0.78; 0.94].

Moreover, Vries et al. [14] developed and compared various ML models for predicting the occurrence of a major osteoporotic fracture (MOF) which consists of fractures that can happen inside bones of the wrist, hip, spine and humerus. The top performing model was used to create a user-friendly application for osteopenia patients to calculate their risk of eventual MOF. Patients visiting a FO-clinic who were above 50 years old were taken into account for the study. Random survival forests RSF, an artificial neural network ANN-DeepSurv model, and Cox regression's discriminative ability (concordance index) were all contrasted to forecast the MOF risk. Missing data was filled in either multiple attributions by enclosed equations or tool of attribution of RSF, and the complete group and a subgroup analyses of patients having osteopenia but without vertebral fracture were carried out. 11% of the patients experienced another MOF. In the entire dataset, Cox regression had a concordance index of 0.697, which was the highest. Cox regression surpassed RSF and ANN-DeepSurv and hence was utilised to create a MOF risk predictor for this type of osteopenia.

3.3 ML in the Sphere of Bone Diseases

For the application of ML in field of Bone diseases, Sharma et al. [16] proposed a study to measure biomarker of bone disease severity i.e. trabecular bone architecture in type GD1 individuals by applying analytics of ML to differentiate between GD patients and healthy ones. Stereological and textural measures STM, were measured by using micro imaging of distal radius of patients with type1 GD and healthy controls (HC). Stereo logical measures explained significant data variation between males and females whereas textural differed between individuals i.e. GD vs HC. An accuracy of 73% of PCA and SVM predictive analysis was achieved.

Similarly, Cheng et al. [17] presented a study to find out the bone mass loss i.e. osteopenia using ML. A sample of adults from a health centre was considered into 3 year stages and the subsequent occurrence of osteopenia was predicted through factors such as demographic, lifestyle, socioeconomic, BMI, MetS scoring index. Feature set was set to algos such as Random Forest RF, Logistic Regression LR, Support Vector Machine SVM, and extreme gradient boosting XG Boost to build predictive models. The XG Boost model showed the best efficiency and performance.

Rastegar et al. [3] proposed a predictive model to identify osteopenia, osteoporosis and normal patients by aid of ML. Data from regions including 4 lumbar and 3 femoral with trochanteric, interochanteric and neck being segmented was included. 4 feature selection methods i.e. classifier attribute evaluation(CLAE) , gain ratio attribute evaluation(GRAE), rule attribute evaluation(ORAE) ,and principle components analysis(PRCA) were used. The classification methods RF, RC, KN and LB classified 4 categories i.e. osteopenia vs normal, osteoporosis vs normal, osteopenia vs osteoporosis and osteoporosis + osteopenia vs osteoporosis under the AUC curve. The highest accuracy was of RF & CLAE in comparison to pairs, RF & ORAE and RF & ORAE in distinguishing between osteoporosis and healthy condition in trochanteric area whereas in neck region RF & PRCA alongwith LB & PRCA, combo gave out the most accuracy.

In the same regards, Wang et al. [18] proposed a predictive model to help identify SRE's (Skeleton related events) in risk groups having Bone metastases (BM) using ML. A group of cancer patients were analysed by using SPSS statistical package and modeller and a predictive model was developed. LR, Decision tree (DT) and SVM were used. The outcome depicted Visual Analog Scale (VAS) of being a key factor to SRE's in LR, DT and SVM with accuracies of 79.2%, 85.8% and 88.2%.

Moreover, Sharma et al. [19] developed a system for classifying and differentiating a bone having cancer from a bone which is normal i.e. healthy on the basis of texture of the affected region by finding the best suited algorithm for detecting the edge and then two sets of features with hog and without hog were put together. Two ML models, SVM and RF were utilised for the features set. The features set comprising of hog outperformed all. The SVM model taught on set of hog feature gave out a score of 0.92 F1 in contrast to Random forest's score of 0.77.

3.4 ML in Aid of Bone Surgery

Chang et al. [22] reviewed that the possibility of AI's usage to develop clinical decisi-on support tools, optimise outcomes of post operation, and enhance technologies being utilised in the operating room has gained immense popularity in bone surgery and machine learning field. The authors first discussed machine learning as a whole and its function in artificial intelligence. They then looked at common ways to apply machine learning, such as classification and regression DT, SVM's, and ANN'S. Finally, the ethical issues involved in the adapting ML for patient care research alongwith the potential future applications of various techniques of ML in the spine surgery field were highlighted.

Additionally, Martin et al. [20] proposed A clinically useful tool for calculating the likelihood that a patient will require a future surgery after hip arthroscopy was created using ML analysis of the arthroscopy registry. A significant result was the likelihood of undergoing a hip arthroscopy 1, 2, or 5 years after the initial procedure. Models which were tested on the data included super learner, random survival forest, Cox elastic and gradient boosted regression GBM. Data was divided into training (75%) group and test (25%)group. The model performance was depicted by the area of the curve. The pre-operative clinical context variables were used for analysis, and all of the several variables comprising the model were used again to compare model performance. 11% was the overall rate of revision. All the models were typically well measured and showed moderate concordance when only pre-operative factors and whole of registry variables were taken into account.

The same was seen when Xie et al. [24] created a model of ML that could simulate decision making and estimate the likelihood of need of surgical operation on the based on the features found in the patient. On the basis of pertinent information from the medical records of patients who presented with lumbar spine complaints a total of 55 indicators were found to predict surgical progression. An Artificial Neural Network predicted surgical candidacy (ANN). The accuracy of the ANN to predict advancement of surgery was 92.1%, and it also had great ability to discriminate (AUC = 0.90), well data fit and good accuracy (AUC = 0.90).

In order to lessen thermal damage during bone drilling, Agarwal et al. [26] suggested a reliable predictive machine-learning (ML) model, and the effectiveness of rotary ultrasonic-assisted bone drilling (RUABD) was experimentally confirmed. On the femur bone of a pig, in vitro tests with varying independent factors were conducted. The most precise prediction models was identified between the multi-linear regression and multi-layer perceptrons, lasso regression, and ridge regression. Model accuracy was predicted using a variety of error metrics, including mean square error (MSE), mean absolute error (MAE) and root mean square error (RMSE). Ridge regression had lower error measures than other ML models. An adequacy of ± 1.7 °C was provided by the Ridge regression model to estimate rise in temperature during drilling operation of bone [29–35].

In addition to demonstrating a promise of sound sensing based on deep learning for error avoidance during surgery, Seibold et al. [25] developed and validated a system suited for detection of drill breakthrough occurrences. Human cadaveric hip specimens were used in an experimental setting to record drill breakthrough sequences with structure-borne audio utilising bespoke piezo contact microphones. It was possible to quickly and accurately create a deep learning technique which automatically detects drill breakthrough occurrences [36–40]. An average sensitivity of 93.64 2.42% was given out by the best variation for drill breakthrough detection [41–43].

4 Conclusions

In the field of orthopaedics, AI is a quite promising tool that will help illuminate an individualised approach and a deeper knowledge of the condition in this age of overwhelming volume of medical field / healthcare data. The performance of ML models for detecting fractures from photos and diagnosing and categorising osteoporosis has showed promise. Another potential area of study is the prediction of fracture risk, and research in this area is being done with the aid of various data sources. Endocrinologists, who are subject-matter specialists, will continue playing a very vital role in identifying unmet clinical requirements to launch the study and interpreting the huge results of the studies to help patients with musculoskeletal illnesses as we approach this methodological turning point. Prognostic surgical outcome models are rapidly entering the orthopaedic industry to help treatment decision making. Classification, object detection, and segmentation are the three most often used ML approaches for evaluating medical pictures, and the right ML algorithms and networks should be selected depending on the study's objectives. Visualising and considering a huge reliance on medical imaging for diagnosis, prognosis and management, research on machine learning in the sphere of orthopaedics is currently lacking despite the substantial consequences it can have on the field. Therefore, machine learning must be prioritised as a tool to retain orthopaedic surgery's leadership status in the musculoskeletal field, even though caution should be given in the implementation of new technologies.

References

1. Kong, S.H., Shin, C.S.: Applications of machine learning in bone and mineral research. Endocrinol. Metab. **36**(5), 928 (2021)
2. Zhang, Z., Sejdić, E.: Radiological images and machine learning: trends, perspectives, and prospects. Comput. Biol. Med. **108**, 354–370 (2019)
3. Rastegar, S., et al.: Radiomics for classification of bone mineral loss: a machine learning study. Diagn. Interv. Imaging **101**(9), 599–610 (2020)
4. Chan, S., Siegel, E.L.: Will machine learning end the viability of radiology as a thriving medical specialty? Br. J. Radiol. **92**(1094), 20180416 (2019)
5. Ko, S., et al.: Artificial intelligence in orthopedics: three strategies for deep learning with orthopedic specific imaging. Knee Surgery, Sports Traumatology, Arthroscopy, 1–4 (2022)
6. Helm, J.M., et al.: Machine learning and artificial intelligence: definitions, applications, and future directions. Curr. Rev. Musculoskelet. Med. **13**(1), 69–76 (2020)
7. Poduval, M., Ghose, A., Manchanda, S., Bagaria, V., Sinha, A.: Artificial intelligence and machine learning: a new disruptive force in orthopaedics. Indian J. Orthopaedics **54**(2), 109–122 (2020)
8. Myint, W.W., Tun, K.S., Tun, H.M.: Analysis on leg bone fracture detection and classification using X-ray images. Machine Learning Res. **3**(3), 49–59 (2018)
9. Yadav, D.P., Sharma, A., Athithan, S., Bhola, A., Sharma, B., Dhaou, I.B.: Hybrid SFNet model for bone fracture detection and classification using ML/DL. Sensors **22**(15), 5823 (2022)
10. Hardalaç, F., et al.: Fracture detection in wrist X-ray images using deep learning- based object detection models. Sensors **22**(3), 1285 (2022)
11. Açıcı, K., Sümer, E., Beyaz, S.: Comparison of different machine learning approaches to detect femoral neck fractures in X-ray images. Heal. Technol. **11**(3), 643–653 (2021)

12. Guan, B., Yao, J., Zhang, G., Wang, X.: Thigh fracture detection using deep learning method based on new dilated convolutional feature pyramid network. Pattern Recogn. Lett. **125**, 521–526 (2019)

13. Cao, Y., Wang, H., Moradi, M., Prasanna, P., Syeda-Mahmood, T.F.: Fracture detection in x-ray images through stacked random forests feature fusion. In: 2015 IEEE 12th international symposium on biomedical imaging (ISBI), pp. 801–805. IEEE (2015)

14. de Vries, B.C.S., Hegeman, J.H., Nijmeijer, W., Geerdink, J., Seifert, C., Groothuis-Oudshoorn, C.G.M.: Comparing three machine learning approaches to design a risk assessment tool for future fractures: predicting a subsequent major osteoporotic fracture in fracture patients with osteopenia and osteoporosis. Osteoporos. Int. **32**(3), 437–449 (2021)

15. Kruse, C., Eiken, P., Vestergaard, P.: Machine learning principles can improve hip fracture prediction. Calcif. Tissue Int. **100**(4), 348–360 (2017)

16. Sharma, G.B., Robertson, D.D., Laney, D.A., Gambello, M.J., Terk, M.: Machine learning based analytics of micro-MRI trabecular bone microarchitecture and texture in type 1 Gaucher disease. J. Biomech. **49**(9), 1961–1968 (2016)

17. Cheng, C.H., Lin, C.Y., Cho, T.H., Lin, C.M.: Machine learning to predict the progression of bone mass loss associated with personal characteristics and a metabolic syndrome scoring index. In: Healthcare, **9**(8), p. 948. MDPI (2021)

18. Wang, Z., Wen, X., Lu, Y., Yao, Y., Zhao, H.: Exploiting machine learning for predicting skeletal-related events in cancer patients with bone metastases. Oncotarget **7**(11), 12612 (2016)

19. Sharma, A., Yadav, D.P., Garg, H., Kumar, M., Sharma, B., Koundal, D.: Bone cancer detection using feature extraction based machine learning model. Computational and Mathematical Methods in Medicine (2021)

20. Martin, R.K., Wastvedt, S., Lange, J., Pareek, A., Wolfson, J., Lund, B.: Limited clinical utility of a machine learning revision prediction model based on a national hip arthroscopy registry. Knee Surgery, Sports Traumatology, Arthroscopy, pp. 1–11 (2022)

21. Saravi, B., et al.: Artificial intelligence-driven prediction modeling and decision making in spine surgery using hybrid machine learning models. J. Personalized Medicine **12**(4), 509 (2022)

22. Chang, M., Canseco, J.A., Nicholson, K.J., Patel, N., Vaccaro, A.R.: The role of machine learning in spine surgery: the future is now. Frontiers in surgery **7**, 54 (2020)

23. Yi, P.H., et al.: Automated detection and classification of shoulder arthroplasty models using deep learning. Skeletal Radiol. **49**(10), 1623–1632 (2020)

24. Xie, N., Wilson, P.J., Reddy, R.: Use of machine learning to model surgical decision-making in lumbar spine surgery. European Spine Journal, pp. 1–7 (2022)

25. Seibold, M., et al.: Real-time acoustic sensing and artificial intelligence for error prevention in orthopedic surgery. Sci. Rep. **11**(1), 1–11 (2021)

26. Agarwal, R., Singh, J., Gupta, V.: An intelligent approach to predict thermal injuries during orthopaedic bone drilling using machine learning. J. Braz. Soc. Mech. Sci. Eng. **44**(8), 1–14 (2022)

27. https://productimages.withfloats.com/serviceimages/actual/620e81b3d640b44d2 e783550FRACTURES

28. https://www.bostonmagazine.com/health/2013/04/04/broken-bone-injury-torn- ligament

29. Bharany, S., et al.: Energy efficient fault tolerance techniques in green cloud computing: A systematic survey and taxonomy. In: Sustainable Energy Technologies and Assessments, Vol. 53, p. 102613. Elsevier BV (2022). https://doi.org/10.1016/j.seta.2022.102613

30. Bharany, S., et al.: Energy-efficient clustering scheme for flying ad-Hoc networks using an optimized LEACH protocol. Energies **14**, 6016 (2021). https://doi.org/10.3390/en14196016

31. Kaur, K., Bharany, S., Badotra, S., Aggarwal, K., Nayyar, A., Sharma, S.: Energy-efficient polyglot persistence database live migration among heterogeneous clouds. In: The Journal of Supercomputing. Springer Science and Business Media LLC (2022). https://doi.org/10.1007/s11227-022-04662-6

32. Bharany, S., Sharma, S., Bhatia, S., Rahmani, M.K.I., Shuaib, M., Lashari, S.A.: Energy efficient clustering protocol for FANETS using moth flame optimization. Sustainability **14**, 6159 (2022). https://doi.org/10.3390/su14106159

33. Bharany, S.; et al.:. A systematic survey on energy-efficient techniques in sustainable cloud computing. Sustainability, **14**, 6256 (2022). https://doi.org/10.3390/su14106256

34. Bharany, S.; et al.: Efficient middleware for the portability of paas services consuming applications among heterogeneous clouds. Sensors **22**, 5013 (2022)

35. Shuaib, M., et al.: A novel optimization for GPU mining using overclocking and undervolting. Sustainability **14**, 8708 (2022). https://doi.org/10.3390/su14148708

36. Bharany, S., et al.: Wildfire monitoring based on energy efficient clustering approach for FANETS. Drones **6**, 193 (2022). https://doi.org/10.3390/drones6080193

37. Singh, P., Dwivedi, Y.K., Kahlon, K.S., Sawhney, R.S., Alalwan, A.A., Rana, N. P.: Smart monitoring and controlling of government policies using social media and cloud computing. Information Systems Frontiers **22**(2), 315-337 (2020)

38. Singh, P., Dwivedi, Y.K., Kahlon, K.S., Pathania, A., Sawhney, R.S.: Can twitter analytics predict election outcome? an insight from 2017 Punjab assembly elections. Government Information Quarterly **37**(2), 101444 (2020)

39. Singh, P., Kahlon, K.S., Sawhney, R.S., Vohra, R., Kaur, S.: Social media buzz created by# nanotechnology: insights from Twitter analytics. Nanotechnology Rev. **7**(6), 521-528 (2018)

40. Singh, P., Sawhney, R.S., Kahlon, K.S.: Sentiment analysis of demonetization of 500- & 1000-rupee banknotes by Indian government. ICT Express **4**(3), 124-129 (2018)

41. Singh, P., Sawhney, R.S., Kahlon, K.S.: Twitter based sentiment analysis of GST implementation by Indian government. In Digital business, pp. 409–427. Springer, Cham (2019). https://doi.org/10.1007/978-3-319-93940-7_17

42. Talwar, B., Arora, A., Bharany, S.: An energy efficient agent aware proactive fault tolerance for preventing deterioration of virtual machines within cloud environment. In: 2021 9th International Conference on Reliability, Infocom Technologies and Optimization (Trends and Future Directions) (ICRITO) (2021)

43. Bharany, S., Sharma, S.: Intelligent green internet of things: an investigation. In Machine Learning, Blockchain, and Cyber Security in Smart Environments, pp. 1–15. Chapman and Hall/CRC

A Machine Learning Framework for Detection of Fake News

Himanshu Gupta[1]($\boxtimes$), Chandni Sharma[1], Swati Arya[2], and Kapil Joshi[3]

[1] Department of Computer Science and Engineering, Quantum University, Roorkee, India
hguptasb@gmail.com
[2] Department of Computer Science and Engineering, College of Engineering Roorkee, Roorkee, India
[3] Department of Computer Science and Engineering, Uttaranchal University, Dehradun, India

Abstract. Any news can spread like wildfire in the current digital era. Many people begin to believe anything they read in various sources without first confirming the veracity of the source. Any false information could lead to rioting among communities and other significant problems. News may spread at very high speed thanks to social media platforms like Twitter, Facebook and other messaging applications like WhatsApp. Therefore, it is essential to identify and stop bogus news in order to maintain social harmony. In order to classify each item into one of the two categories true or spurious, authors used machine learning-based algorithms. For this dataset of 20800 records from Kaggle that contains both real and phoney news, was used to train the various machine learning algorithms. SVM, Random Forest, Passive Aggressive Classifier, Decision Tree, logistic regression and KNN are the six machine learning-based classifiers used to identify fake news, with SVM achieving the greatest accuracy of 92.9 percent.

Keywords: SVM · PAC · TFIDF · Decision tree · Machine learning

1 Introduction

The most fascinating and significant aspect of everyone's life is news. Every single piece of news has a significant impact on one's life. Regardless of how large, it must be the case. Fake refers to false information or content. Any form of manipulated news can have a significant impact on the majority of the population. Nowadays, social media platforms are accessible to everyone, and a website's page ranking is based on how many people visit it. In the past, traditional news was reliable and compiled from reliable sources. The news could only be published through a few outlets. However, as the digital world develops, more and more content is accessible online. It raises the likelihood of original data being manipulated [1]. It can result in news that is inaccurate.

The most widely used and least expensive method of public communication is social media. There are numerous ways to communicate, including on YouTube, WhatsApp, Facebook, Twitter, and Instagram, among others.

Social media is becoming a more popular place for people to find and read news because it is the quickest and least expensive method. The phrase "fake news" has no

R. Singh et al. (Eds.): ICBDA 2022, CCIS 1742, pp. 64–78, 2022.
https://doi.org/10.1007/978-3-031-23647-1_6

clear definition, nevertheless. False information that leads to misunderstandings about a person or circumstance is known as fake news. Authenticity and intent are the two essential characteristics to meet the definition. First, false information that can be proven to be untrue is included in fake news.

Second, fake information is produced in order to mislead readers. It was also discovered that now social media is performing better than traditional media (television, newspaper) as the primary news source. [2]. Another study discovered that towards the end of the election of a powerful country US for the post of president, tweets over 1 million had been flooded in the social media and was associated with the fake news "Pizzagate." [3]. This incident became so popular that time that this term "fake news" becomes the buzz word. Actually in today's scenario many bots can be employed to continuously post bogus news on the social media platform which can disturb the social harmony badly. As a result, timely detection of such an event is critical. So that competent authority can take timely action in order to avoid any loss caused by such news.

A Recent activity that has been notified in July 2022, in which an Indian politician Nupur Sharma commented on some religious issue spread so fast on social media that it disturbed the social harmony and many cities faced riots which claimed many lives. Despite so many benefits of modern social media, reliability of news on social media is steadily declining. Because it is quicker and simpler to distribute news online through social media, fake news and news pieces that purposefully contain incorrect information are crafted online for many reasons, including political and financial benefit. Detecting these types of news is very much important for the sake of the community, as it is becoming menace to the society.

It would be a better idea if we could validate the content first and then allow that validated content to publish on the social media. In this article, we will assess the veracity of the news or content by answering yes for genuine content and false for fake content. Many popular machine learning algorithms are used in this article for this purpose [4].

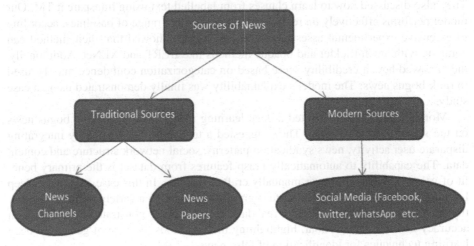

Fig. 1. Various sources of news

Figure 1 depicts the various news sources we use in our daily lives to stay up to date on world events. We can divide news sources into two broad categories: traditional and modern. Traditional sources are typically the source of authentic news, whereas because anyone can post on modern media like facebook etc, the authenticity of news from such sources is always suspected.

2 Literature Review

Considering the significance of false news detection for maintaining social harmony many researchers proposed their methods for detection of fake news in different social sites.

Kai Shu et al. [2] characterised and detected fake news during the characterization phase, In both social and traditional media, they introduced the basic theory and concepts of fake news. They analysed existing data mining-based methods for de- tecting false news during the detection phase, including feature extraction and model building. The datasets, evaluation measures, and interesting future paths in false news identification were also discussed. One significant work in this direction is proposed by Wang et.al [3] they revealed a new data set called LIAR for the automatic detection of false news. LIAR is comparatively much larger than previous datasets, allowing for the development of computational methods for detecting fake news. LIAR's authentic; real-world brief comments from various circumstances and diverse speakers enable research into developing a comprehensive false news detector. He showed how text and meta-data may be used to significantly increase the accuracy of fake news identification. Future research into the activity of automatic fact-checking over knowledge bases is also possible, given the detailed analysis report and source documents links in this dataset.

Bhattarai et al. [5] proposed a framework for identifying false news using the Tsetlin Machine (TM) that is clear and easy to understand. Clauses are used in their TM architecture to collect lexical and semantic characteristics based on document word patterns. They also discussed how to learn clauses from labelled text using transparent TM. Our model performs effectively on real-world datasets with a range of baselines, according to extensive experimental assessments. Their research showed that their method can compete with much trickier and opaque methods like BERT and XLNet. Additionally, they showed how a credibility score based on categorization confidence may be used to rank bogus news. The model's explainability was finally demonstrated using a case study.

Monti et al. [6] demonstrated a deep learning method for identifying bogus news on the social network Twitter. They suggested a technique for seamlessly integrating disparate user activity, news syndication patterns, social network structure and content data. The capability to automatically grasp features from dataset is the primary benefit of using deep learning over manually crafted features. In this case, geometric deep learning was chosen because the data is graph-structured. In a variety of difficult situations involving massive amounts of real data, their model demonstrated extremely high accuracy and robust behaviour, highlighting the enormous promise of geometric deep learning techniques for identification of false news.

Fakeddit, a brand-new dataset for studying fake news, was introduced by Nakamura et al. [7]. Fakeddit has much larger samples of multidimentional nature with many labels for different levels of categorization than previous datasets. They carried out a number of experiments with various standard algorithms and performed various performance analyses on It., emphasizing the significance of Fakeddit's big-scale multimodality and showing that there is still much possibility for advancement in the area of detection of false news. Their datasets has numerous applications in the study of fake news and other fields of study. Nevertheless, they did not make advantage of user comments and submission metadata.

In order to help individuals distinguish between fake and true news, Kudariet et al. [8] conducted a study on the fake news identification problem in online social networks (including phoney tweets, posts, and subjects). Our goal is to simultaneously identify bogus news from online social networks based on a variety of information sources, including textual content, profiles, and descriptions as well as the relationships between authors and article subjects.

Beihang et.al [9] Concerns have recently been expressed about the proliferation of fake news throughout the world. There could be serious repercussions from these false political reports. It is becoming more crucial to identify fake news. In their study, the authors developed a single model, called TI-CNN, that can merge text and image data with the relevant explicit and latent properties. Strong expandability makes the suggested model quickly able to incorporate more news aspects. Additionally, a CNN deep learning method allows the model to see the entire input at once and trains significantly more quickly than an LSTM or many other RNN models. On the data gathered before the election, they ran experiments. TI-CNN can successfully identify bogus news, according to the testing results. Similarly [10, 11] also used deep learning based method for classifying a news into one of the two categories.

3   Methodology

3.1   Dataset Description

False news datasets can be compiled from a variety of sources, including news organizations, websites, and social media sources such as whatsApp, Facebook, twitter and others. Because manually separating the various types of news is difficult As a result, there is a need for an expert narrator who can evaluate the arguments, supporting data, and historical context from credible sources. In general, news information can be gathered through a variety of methods, including reporters, fact-checking portals, and crowd source employees. There are currently no concurrent standard datasets for detection of fake news issues.

The dataset (a false news article.CSV file) obtained from kaggel.com is utilised in this paper. About 20,800 records from various online articles make up this dataset, and they include the following characteristics: (text, author, title, and label). The preprocessing procedure increased the dataset's size to 20,761 records. 10,423 pieces of actual news and 10,432 pieces of fraudulent news were sorted into two categories using this data. In this work, only two features—text and label—are utilised to identify bogus news. Real news is represented by label one, while unreliable (or fraudulent) news is represented by label zero (Figs. 2, 3).

Unnamed: 0		title	text	label
0	8476	You Can Smell Hillary's Fear	Daniel Greenfield, a Shillman Journalism Fello...	FAKE
1	10294	Watch The Exact Moment Paul Ryan Committed Pol...	Google Pinterest Digg Linkedin Reddit Stumbleu...	FAKE
2	3608	Kerry to go to Paris in gesture of sympathy	U.S. Secretary of State John F. Kerry said Mon...	REAL
3	10142	Bernie supporters on Twitter erupt in anger ag...	— Kaydee King (@KaydeeKing) November 9, 2016 T...	FAKE
4	875	The Battle of New York: Why This Primary Matters	It's primary day in New York and front-runners...	REAL

Fig. 2. Snapshot of dataset

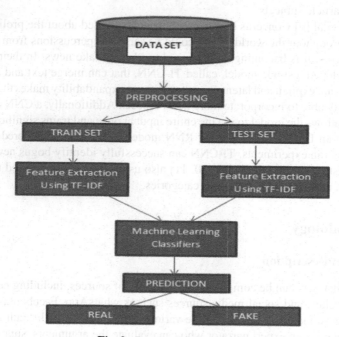

Fig. 3. Proposed methodology

3.2 Feature Extraction Using TF-IDF

This is the most crucial aspect of the methodology. Following the preprocessing step, the entire dataset is divided into two parts: the train dataset and the test dataset. Typically, the test data set is 10-20% of the total dataset, with the remainder used for training. The most important step after dividing the dataset into two parts and before applying any machine learning algorithm for classification of news into one of two categories, i.e. real or fake, is determining how important a phrase is in a given set of words. The Term frequency-Inverse term frequency methods assign weight to words based on their importance. The frequency with which a term appears in the document determines its importance.

TF-IDF consists of two terms. TF is an acronym for Term Frequency and IDF is Inverse Document Frequency. This study employed TF-IDF [12, 13] to determine the relevance of a word in a set of text. The occurrences of a term in the text compensates for the increase in meaning that occurs when an entry in the message appears more frequently (data-set). The frequency represents the occurances of a specific word comes in any particular document. As can be seen, it makes sense that as a word appears in the text, it becomes more relevant. Because the sequence of terms is unimportant, a vector can be used to explain the term in the pack of words.

For every distinct term in the essay,

tf(t,d) = count of t in document / number of words in document

TF is the frequency counter of word, and df, or document frequency, is the number of appearance of the term in the document set N. The IDF method evaluates a word's relevance.

idf(t) = N/ df(t) = N/N(t)

df(t) = Number of times t appear in document idf(t) = N/ df(t) = N/N(t)

idf(t) = log(N/ df(t)) where,

df(t) = frequency of word (t) in document

N(t) = The number of documents that contain the term t tf-idf(t, d) = tf(t, d)idf(t)

Tf-idf is a great metric for determining how important a phrase is to a passage in a series or corpus. The tf-idf weighting technique assigns a weight to each word in a document based on how frequently its terms are used (tf) and the document's inverse frequency (tf) (idf). Higher weighted words are thought to be more significant. The tf-idf weights typically include Normalized Term Frequency (tf) and Inverse Document Frequency (idf).

3.3 Machine Learning Models

Support Vector Machine
SVM is an acronym for support vector machine it is also known as the support vector network, comes under the category of supervised learning method. SVM can solve both classification and regression type of tasks. However, its main uses in machine learning are to solve classification problems. The SVM algorithm's central idea is to find the hyperplane that is the best line or decision boundary for classifying n-dimensional space. The hyperplane assists in quickly categorising future data points. [14, 15]

Logistic Regression
Logistic Regression is a widely used classification technique for solving problems having two output classes. Because linear regression is ineffective for classification, logistic regression is used to solve classification problems. Though it works best with binary classification problems, such as whether incoming mail is spam or not, or whether a customer will buy insurance based on certain parameters it can be generalized to solve

multiclass problems also. Logistic regression computes the probability of an event and thus produces a value between 0 and 1.

Decision Tree Classifier

The decision tree [16] is one of the best machine learning classifiers that can be used to solve various classification problems. As the name suggest it has tree like structure. We start from the roots and as per the conditions required to solve the classification problems, its branches are created in the last the leaf node represents the result or class label. So in order to reach to the leaf node we need to traverse through the branches which represents conditions according to the result of those condition further traversing through the tree is done and in the last leaf node as already discussed represents the class label.

Random Forest

Random Forest machine learning algorithm [17] is the example of ensemble learning based algorithms. It can be used to solve problems involving regression and classification. It falls under the umbrella of supervised learning. In this case, we create many decision trees, and each tree predicts the output; ultimately, the majority wins, the majority decision of the trees is chosen as the final output. Because this algorithm takes less time in training than other algorithms, we use it in this paper to accurately predict output. Even when data is scarce, this can be used. Random forest, which constructs a large number of de-correlated trees before averaging them, is a significant improvement over bagging.

4   Result and Analysis

Six popular machine learning models are used to differentiate between fake and real news. Table 1 gives the performance of passive aggressive classifier and the same is represented graphically by Fig 4. In the same way Table 2 gives the performance of logistic regression classifier, Table 3 gives performance of support vector machine, Table 4 gives performance of Random forest classifier, Table 5 gives performance of Decision Tree and Table 6 gives performance of KNN. The Performance of above mentioned classifiers are also given graphically in Fig 5, Fig 6, Fig 7, Fig 8 and Fig 9 respectively.

Further the accuracy of all the six classifiers are compared in Table 7 and graphically represented by Fig 10 similarly the Precision, Recall and F1-Score of various algorithms are compared and represented graphically by Fig 11, Fig 12 and Fig 13 respectively.

Table 1. Passive aggressive classifier

	Precision	Recall	f1-score	Support
FAKE	93	92	93	638
REAL	92	93	93	629

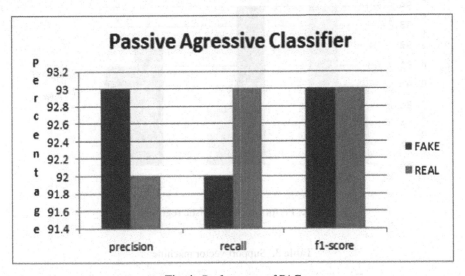

Fig. 4. Performance of PAC

Table 2. Logistic regression

	Precision	Recall	f1-score	Support
FAKE	90	94	92	638
REAL	94	89	91	629

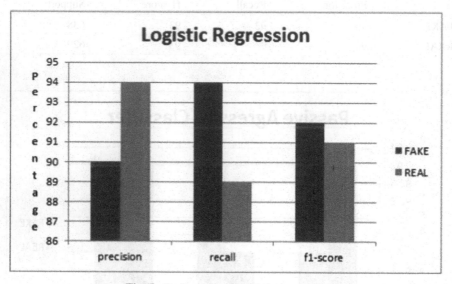

Fig. 5. Performance of logistic regression

Table 3. Support vector machine

	Precision	Recall	f1-score	Support
FAKE	91	95	93	638
REAL	95	91	93	629

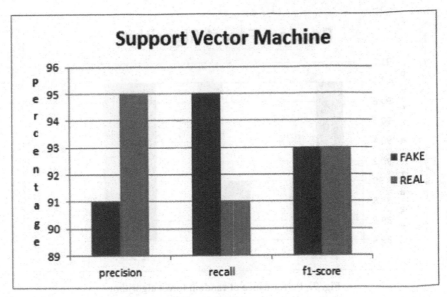

Fig. 6. Performance of support vector machine

Table 4. Random forest classifier

FAKE	Precision	Recall	f1-score	Support
	91	90	91	638
REAL	90	91	91	629

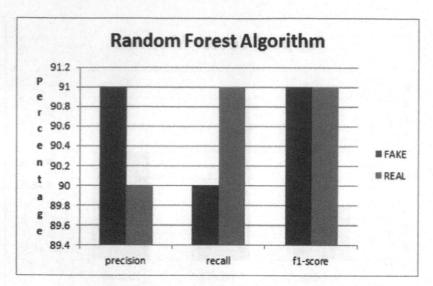

Fig. 7. Performance of random forest algorithm

Table 5. Decision tree classifier

	Precision	Recall	f1-score	Support
FAKE	81	82	81	638
REAL	81	80	81	629

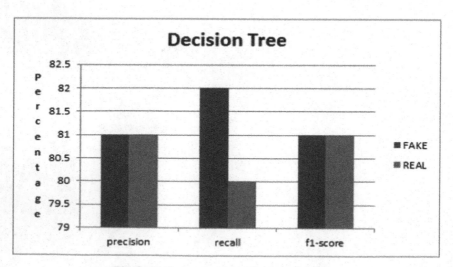

Fig. 8. Performance of decision tree algorithm

Table 6. K nearest neighbor

FAKE	Precision 81	Recall 90	f1-score 85	Support 638
REAL	88	79	83	629

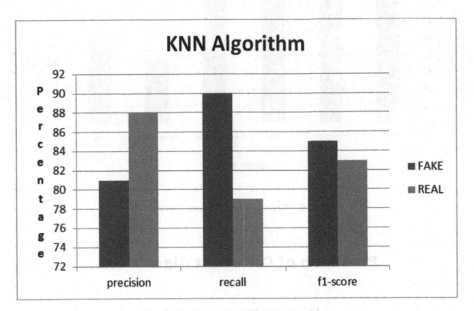

Fig. 9. Performance of KNN algorithm

Table 7. Accuracy of different classifiers

S.NO	Algorithm	Accuracy
1	PAC	92.82
2	Logistic Regression	91.71
3	SVM	92.9
4	Random Forest	91
5	Decision Tree	81.61
6	K Nearest Neighbour	84.45

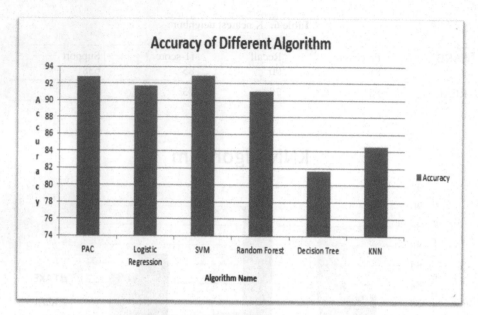

Fig. 10. Accuracy of different algorithm

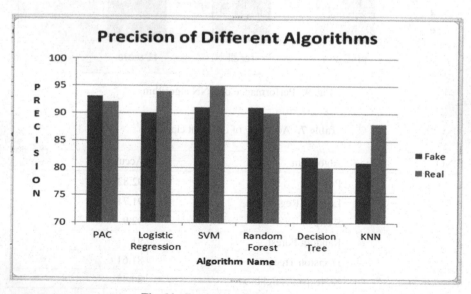

Fig. 11. Precison of different algorithm

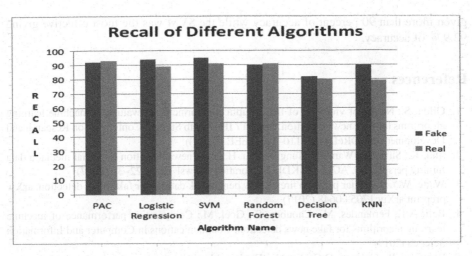

Fig. 12. Recall of different algorithm

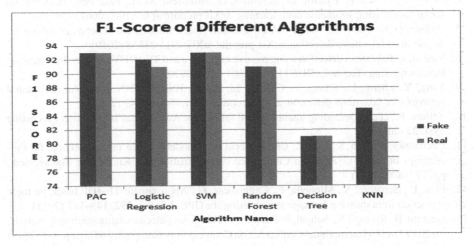

Fig. 13. F1-Score of different algorithm

5 Conclusion

Today, when telecom companies are testing 5G and the IT sector is booming, any news can quickly spread thanks to various social media platforms. Fake or bogus news can have a negative impact on society. We have seen numerous instances where fake news has disrupted social harmony. The importance of fake news detection is universally acknowledged. Because manual checking of all news articles floating around the internet is not possible, technology plays an important role here. Many artificial intelligence-based algorithms are used to solve problems like classifying email as spam or not spam. The authors used six popular machine learning algorithms in this study to classify news into two categories: fake and real, and they discovered that out of six four algorithms given more than 90 percent of accuracy while the SVM was the most effective giving 92.9 % of accuracy.

References

1. Gilda, S.: Notice of violation of IEEE publication principles: evaluating machine learning algorithms for fake news detection. In: 2017 IEEE 15th Student Conference on Research and Development (SCOReD), pp. 110–115. IEEE ((2017))
2. Shu, K., Sliva, A., Wang, S., Tang, J., Liu, H.: Fake news detection on social media: a data mining perspective. ACM SIGKDD Explorations Newsl 19(1), 22–36 (2017)
3. Wang, W.Y.: Liar, liar pants on fire: A new benchmark dataset for fake news detection. arXiv preprint arXiv:1705.00648 (2017)
4. Bali, A.P., Fernandes, M., Choubey, S., Goel, M.: Comparative performance of machine learning algorithms for fake news detection. Communications in Computer and Information Science (2019)
5. Bhattarai, B., Granmo, O.C., Jiao, L.: Explainable tsetlin machine framework for fake news detection with credibility score assessment. arXiv preprint arXiv:2105.09114 (2021)
6. Monti, F., Frasca, F., Eynard, D., Mannion, D., Bronstein, M.M.: Fake news detection on social media using geometric deep learning. arXiv preprint arXiv:1902.06673 (2019)
7. Nakamura, K., Levy, S., Wang, W.Y.: r/fakeddit: A new multimodal benchmark dataset for fine-grained fake news detection. arXiv preprint arXiv:1911.03854 (2019)
8. Kudari, J.: Fake news detection using passive aggressive and TF-IDF Vectorizer. International Research J. Eng. Technol. (IRJET) 7(9), 1601-1603 (2020)
9. Yang, Y., Zheng, L., Zhang, J., Cui, Q., Li, Z., Yu, P.S.: TI-CNN: Convolutional neural networks for fake news detection. arXiv preprint arXiv:1806.00749 (2018)
10. Zellers, R., et al.: Defending against neural fake news. Adv. Neural Information Processing Syst. 32 (2019)
11. Ruchansky, N., Seo, S., Liu, Y.: Csi: a hybrid deep model for fake news detection. In: Proceedings of the 2017 ACM on Conference on Information and Knowledge Management, pp. 797–806 (2017)
12. Erra, U., Senatore, S., Minnella, F., Caggianese, G.: Approximate TF–IDF based on topic extraction from massive message stream using the GPU. Inf. Sci. 292, 143–161 (2015)
13. Bhutani, B., Rastogi, N., Sehgal, P., Purwar, A.: Fake news detection using sentiment analysis. In: 2019 Twelfth International Conference on Contemporary Computing (IC3), pp. 1–5 (2019)
14. ElAzab, A.: Fake accounts detection in twitter based on minimum weighted feature. World (2016)
15. Aylien, N.B.: Support vector machines: a simple explanation. KD Nuggets 1, 1–5 (2016)
16. Fletcher, S., Islam, M.Z.: Decision tree classification with differential privacy: a survey. ACM Computing Surveys (CSUR) 52(4), 1–33 (2019)
17. Natarajan, R., et al.: Intelligent gravitational search random forest algorithm for fake news detection. Int. J. Mod. Phys. C 33(06), 2250084 (2022)

Author Index